THE PASSIONATE NOMAD

THE
PASSIONATE NOMAD

The Diary of Isabelle Eberhardt

Beacon Press   Boston

Beacon Press
25 Beacon Street
Boston, Massachusetts 02108

Beacon Press books
are published under the auspices of
the Unitarian Universalist Association of Congregations.

English translation ©1987 by Nina de Voogd
Foreword and notes ©1987 by Rana Kabbani

First published as a Beacon paperback in 1988
by arrangement with Virago Press Limited

95 94 93 92 91 90 89 88   1 2 3 4 5 6 7 8

Library of Congress Cataloging-in-Publication Data

Eberhardt, Isabelle, 1877–1904.
The passionate nomad.
(Virago/Beacon travelers)
1. Eberhardt, Isabelle, 1877–1904—Diaries.
2. Women—Algeria—Biography. 3. Algeria—Biography.
I. Kabbani, Rana.   II. Title.   III. Series.
DT294.7.E2A3   1988   965'.03'0924   87-42854
ISBN 0-8070-7103-X (pbk.)

INTRODUCTION

Oisive jeunesse
à tout asservie, Par délicatesse
j'ai perdu ma vie – Rimbaud,
'Chanson de la plus haut tour'

Isabelle Eberhardt, since her death at the age of twenty-eight in that startling flash flood at Aïn Sefra, has come to be seen as a highly romantic figure, touched with the dark hues of *fin du siècle* decadence. The eccentric and contradictory details of her life, viewed as they were in retrospect, only added to the mystique: a woman disguised as a man, an aristocrat living the life of a beggar, a sensualist haunted by the soul, and a transgressor in the best Byronic tradition.

But she was a modern figure, not a romantic one. Her ailments and obsessions were prematurely those of the 1960s, and hardly related at all to the sensibilities of her own era.

She must have suffered from our contemporary complaint, anorexia – which most often plagues young women – since a great many of its symptoms are remarkable in her physical and psychological constitution. She was painfully thin, completely flat-chested, with decayed teeth, an abundance of bodily hair, and no periods (these particular physiological characteristics, which many anorexics develop, made it easier for her to pass as a man). She was constantly depressed, often suicidal, and suffered from recurring bouts of mental debility and from an overriding and self-destructive promiscuity.

The drugs she began taking in late adolescence (following the example of her two half-brothers, Nicolas and Augustin, who no doubt initiated her in their abuse) could not have done much to help her already unstable nerves.

For the rest of her life, Isabelle would remain severely dependent on narcotics and on alchohol; in North Africa, she would function for days without sustenance, as long as she had enough *kif* and *arak* to stun herself with. Every last borrowed franc was spent on these habits, for she had the makings of a hardened addict – the loss of all will power, of all sense of reality and self-respect.

The voyage East for Isabelle was primarily a gateway to sex, as it had been and would be for countless other Europeans. It provided a way of attaining experiences more varied than those she could have expected in suburban Geneva. It satisfied her craving for adventure, her delight in disguise, as well as her sexual curiosity. Like the majority of Europeans who made this voyage of self-discovery, she carried with her a great deal of mental baggage, especially that stereotypical notion of the East as a coffer of erotic delights and unlimited freedoms.

Like Flaubert, who was finally able to shake off the moral restrictions of Rouen when he engaged Cairene prostitutes; like André Gide or T.E. Lawrence, who only managed to come out of their respective closets when they solicited the services of Arab boys; or like those endless droves of Western hippies who landed in India in the sixties and seventies, a paperback copy of *The Karma Sutra* in hand to elucidate the mysteries of 'Eastern' sex, and to assist them in 'letting it all hang out' (much to the embarrassment, the hilarity or the anger of the local people), Isabelle Eberhardt's North African voyage was a sexual trip in the contemporary sense of the word. It was a trip that offered erotic as well as narcotic highs; so much so that the place itself became slightly irrelevant to her purposes – she could just as well have been in Kashmir or Katmandu.

And like those hippies who left affluent middle-class homes to rough it in the East, arriving quite destitute and throwing themselves on the mercy of such impoverished communities as were unsuspecting enough to take them in, Isabelle went slumming when she went to North Africa. On her second trip there she landed with practically no money at all, having been irresponsible and impatient enough to quit Geneva without first sorting out her inheritance. This, had it been handled properly, would have assured her a private income for life. Instead, she fled to Algeria with a few books and a change of clothes, leaving a financial transaction of such magnitude and of such importance to her future prospects in the most untrustworthy hands imaginable.

Once in North Africa, she began sinking into a penury from which, given her impractical and somewhat hysterical nature, she was incapable of ever again emerging. She slept wrapped in her dirty burnous in public gardens or in the houses of acquaintances; she arranged her social calls to coincide with meal-times, knowing that she would certainly be asked, in accordance with the custom of Arab hospitality, to remain and share food. She fell into debt with the local shopkeepers, was unable to pay her servant, and eventually took to begging, a few francs at a time, to buy more drink and drugs.

Unadapted to practical life, she nevertheless had a manic desire for financial security (even though she had neglectfully destroyed her chances of ever actually achieving it). Despising toil, she settled for the most menial labour, since she could not rouse herself enough to seek employment more in keeping with her true abilities. Unable to learn from experience, she repeated the same mistakes over and over again till they became the determining pattern of her entire existence. Her natural despondency could only have been aggravated by her incapacity to help herself.

She was a vagabond, a wanderer, not only because of frenzied boredom and innate restlessness, but because she actually had no real roots anywhere, and therefore belonged nowhere. The product of an eccentric, exiled family which had settled somewhat haphazardly on the outskirts of Geneva, while remaining completely isolated from the neighbouring community, Isabelle grew up believing herself to be the daughter of a deceased Russian nobleman, not imagining for a moment that her actual father was that very Trophimovsky whom she called 'Vava' (or Great-Uncle), whose advances she might well have suffered, and whose lunatic domination crushed them all.

Like Rimbaud, whose life and whose inner conflicts seem to parallel her own, Isabelle suffered from a profound sense of *dépaysement*. 'I have given up the hope of ever having a corner on earth to call my own; a home, a family, peace or prosperity,' she wrote in her journal, almost echoing the poet's own poignant cry, when, prematurely aged, ill, his leg amputated and his mind tortured by endless financial worries, he felt life closing in on him: 'Adieu mariage, adieu famille, adieu avenir! Ma vie est passée. Je ne suis plus qu' un tronçon immobile.'

And like Rimbaud, whose only deliverance from the stifling atmosphere of the bourgeois home in Charleville which he so vehemently hated came when he buried himself in Africa, gun-running for the Abyssinians, Isabelle fled from her 'season in hell' at the Villa Neuve into a physical and moral desert from which there was no turning back.

Both she and Rimbaud represented existential breakdown; they were a metaphor depicting the moral collapse of the European in the East. Even though they both affected to despise the priveted world of the *colons* which rejected them anyway, and set up house with local spouses, they still functioned within and ultimately served the designs of colonialism.

Rimbaud profited from his trade in the goods of empire, in skins, ivory, gold, guns and slaves, becoming part and parcel of the imperial transaction; while Eberhardt, who had penetrated into the North African religious confraternities in her capacity as a Muslim convert, was happy to share her insider's information when it was found that it could help the French colonial authorities expand their sphere of influence and crush nationalist unrest.

Always an apologist for French rule, even when she suffered expulsion from French territories, Isabelle could not perceive a North Africa free from European domination. When pressed to write about incidents of nationalist uprising, such as the case of the Marguerite rebels, she demurred, perhaps not wishing to offend the French or align herself too closely with Arab aspirations.

The resistance movement (the *maquis*, as it was called) had long been underway, and its great nationalist hero, 'Abd al-Kader al-Jazairi, was the son of the Sheikh of the Kadrya confraternity to which Isabelle had been admitted; indeed, his message had been spread through the instantly available religious network which bore him allegiance. After his exile and death, the struggle continued. But Isabelle's journals reveal nothing of this political ferment; she either chose to ignore it, or she was actually not fully aware of it, having had dealings only with those Algerians who collaborated with or were in the employ of the French. She lived in that grey area where two distinct worlds – that of the coloniser and that of the colonised – coincided uneasily.

Because Isabelle Eberhardt willed herself to adopt a male persona – she gave herself a man's name ('Si Mahmoud'), dressed in a man's garb, frequented a man's world – she deliberately put a distance between herself and other women. Her perceptions were affected by this; she became a mouthpiece for patriarchy, voicing traditional male views on sex, culture, religion and politics. Perhaps this position gave her a sense of power; after all, many woman travellers adopted a similar stance, thereby hoping to win acceptance as token men. Even though powerless and dispossessed in their own countries, these women often felt, when crossing into other cultures, that the codes and laws that restricted local women (often identical to the codes and laws that they had been restricted by at home) were not applicable to and did not limit them.

In Isabelle Eberhardt's case, the situation was slightly more complicated. Her dressing as an Arab man (a two-fold masquerade, since she was posing both a *man* and as an *Arab*) exiled her completely from the society of Arab women, who were socially sequestered from male company. Although no one for a moment supposed that she was either male or Arab, courtesy nevertheless required that this pretence of hers be respected. She, in turn, was aware that the formal codes of etiquette implicit in this segregation of the sexes were to be upheld. This would have suited her perfectly, since she hadn't the slightest desire to associate with women, for whom she felt only dislike and hostility.

Her disguise endeared her to no one. Arab women must have thought her a pitiful and uncouth creature for mixing in male circles which were better left alone; Arab men must have found her ambivalent persona rather trying and her sexual presumptions perverse. French women would have been contemptuous of her for having de-classed and de-sexed and de-raced herself. She was untouchable as far as they were concerned. French men would have shared the view of their women, while also perceiving her as a dangerous symbol of female rebellion; her taking Arab lovers would have galled them too, for in a colonial society, miscegenation – if it occurred between a white woman and a non-white man (rather than vice-versa) – was considered a deadly sin. One French military man, Captain Cauvet, was scandalised when, informed that a lady wished to see him, he had encountered a slender young Arab whom he had taken for the servant of the lady in question, but who had turned out to be Isabelle herself. Ambiguity of this kind was dangerous enough in itself, and constituted a political liability.

Could Isabelle Eberhardt, given the limitations of her personality and of her political awareness, have judged the colonial climate any differently, have foreseen its conse-quences any better? Only five decades after her death the whole of Algeria would be knee-deep in bloodshed; the French *colons* she had so heartily defended would be-come the fiercest of torturers, whose kindliest cliché was 'Pas d'humanité pour les Arabes.' And those shadowy local women she had despised and ignored would produce daughters whose bravery would astonish the world; hero-ines such as Djamila Boupacha who was deflowered with a bottle by her French captors and subjected to countless other outrages; or Djamila Bouhired who was disfigured by the tortures she endured but who inspired a whole generation of resistance fighters to hide their guns beneath their veils, transforming the harem world into headquarters for guerrilla activity.

Perhaps farsightedness of this sort was historically im-possible, especially for one who saw North Africa through a haze of literary clichés. Isabelle, like countless other Europeans, had come to the Orient on the flying-carpet of Orientalism; her notions of the place had already been determined by her early readings of the works of Gautier, Baudelaire, and Loti.

In any case her odyssey was an inward, not an outward

one. She explored the state of her psyche rather than that of the country. The reader becomes familiar, perhaps overly familiar, with her moods and fears, but hardly learns anything about the domestic or social or political dimension of her life. She may have been too depressed or too drugged or too *distraite* to offer such a portrait, but from the rare snatches in her diary where she describes things or persons outside of herself (as, for example, in her description of impoverished workers in Marseilles), one cannot help feeling a tremendous sense of waste, as one would have liked many more such acute observations to have come to us from her pen.

The real tragedy of Isabelle Eberhardt was that she was so consumed by her passions and her moods, so very much the victim of her own mishandling of her talent, that she never arrived at her true potential as a writer. Perhaps if she had lived longer, if she had survived the ravaging years of her second decade, she could have mustered the emotional strength to harmonise between her many warring selves.

Although her death was an accidental one, it somehow takes on the poignancy of a suicide. One can just picture her lying under the fatal timbers, the way the rescue workers must have found her, weighted down by her full clothes like a travesty of an Ophelia, 'the hoar leaves' of the tattered notebooks of her diary swollen by water as their entries had been swollen by tears.

In editing these diaries, I have found it best to delete such passages as seemed unjustifiably repetitious, as well as most of the poems or the bits of prose that Isabelle copied out from books in order to re-read later without having actually to carry weighty volumes around with her. Although the great bulk of the diaries was written in French, the entries she made in Russian are preceded by a cross (✝), while those made in Arabic are preceded by a crescent (☽). References to people or places or incidents that appear opaque have been explained in the notes at the end, which are folllowed by a glossary of Arabic terms.

In introducing these diaries, I have been inspired by Cecily Mackworth's biography, *The Destiny of Isabelle Eberhardt* (London; Quartet Books, 1977), and by Henry

Miller's study of Rimbaud, *The Time of the Assassins* (London; Quartet, 1984). I have also benefited from illuminating conversations with Annette Kobak, Isabelle's most recent and most thorough biographer, and with Khaled Kaak, of the Tunisian Embassy in London, who offered invaluable assistance with words in the North African dialects.

Rana Kabbani
London 1987

JOURNAL ONE

Isabelle records her thoughts during her visit to her newly married brother Augustin in Sardinia.

Cagliari, 1 January 1900

I sit here all by myself, looking at the grey expanse of murmuring sea ... I am utterly *alone* on earth, and always will be in this Universe so full of lures and disappointments ... *alone*, turning my back on a world of dead hopes and memories.

The torments and confusion of the last six months have tempered my soul for good, and I can now face the worst of time, even death or destruction, without turning a hair. The knowledge I have acquired of the human heart is now so keen that I know the two months ahead will only bring me more sorrow, for I simply pay no attention to anything other than the dreams that make up my *true* personality. I seem to wear a mask that bespeaks someone cynical, dissipated ... No one so far has ever managed to see through it and catch a glimpse of the sensitive soul which lives behind it.

No one has ever understood that even though I may seem to be driven by the senses alone, my heart is in fact a pure one filled with love and tenderness, and with boundless compassion for all who suffer injustice, all who are weak and oppressed ... a heart both proud and unswerving in its commitment to Islam, a cause for which I long to give my life some day.

I shall dig in my heels and go on acting the lunatic in the intoxicating expanse of desert as I did last summer, or go on galloping through olive groves in the Tunisian Sahel, as I did in the autumn.

1

Those silent nights again, those lazy rides on horse-back through the salty plains of the Oued Righ's and the Oued Souf's white sands! That feeling, sad and bliss-ful at once, that would fill my pariah's heart every time I struck camp surrounded by friends, among Spahis and nomads, none of whom ever considered me the despic-able outcast I had so miserably become at the hands of fate.

Right now, I long for one thing only: to lead that life again in Africa ... to sleep in the chilly silence of the night below stars that drop from great heights, with the sky's infinite expanse for a roof and the warm earth for a bed, in the knowledge that no one pines for me *anywhere on earth*, that there is no place where I am being missed or expected. To know that is to be free and unencumbered, a nomad in the great desert of life where I shall never be anything but an outsider. Such is the only form of bliss, however bitter, the Mektoub will ever grant me, but then happiness of the sort coveted by all of frantic humanity, will never be mine.

The light went out of my life when, two years ago, my white dove lay down to sleep in Bône's Cimetière des Croyants.[1]

Now that Vava has returned to dust as well, and nothing is left of all that once seemed so solid and so permanent, now that all is gone, vanished, for all time and eternity! ... and now that fate has so curiously, so mysteriously driven a wedge between myself and the only being who ever came close enough to my true nature to catch however pale a glimpse of it, Augustin ... [2]

And now that ... Enough! I must put all those recent events to rest once and for all.

I am here out of friendship for the man Fate put across my path,[3] just as I was in the midst of a crisis – ☾ *please Allah*, may it be the last one.

My feeling of friendship is all the stronger for it.

As a nomad who has no country besides Islam and neither family nor close friends, I shall wend my way through life until it is time for that everlasting sleep inside the grave ...

MAHMOUD ESSADI

Cagliari, 7 January 1900
Impressions in a park,
around 5 p.m.

A savage landscape, the jagged outlines of deeply gutted hills either reddish or grey in colour, cavalcades of maritime pines and Barbary fig trees. Greenery so lush it is almost out of place in the heart of winter. Salt lagoons with surfaces the colour of lead, dead and immobile like desert shotts.

And up there at the very top the town's silhouette straddles the steep hillside. Ancient ramparts and a square old tower, different levels of roofs, all cast in a pink hue against a sky of indigo.

Near the very top, barracks identical to the ones in Algeria, long and low in shape with red-tiled roofs and flaky, peeling walls. Dark old churches full of statues and mosaics, objects of great luxury in a country where poverty is the rule. Vaulted passageways that make for resounding footsteps and booming echoes. A maze of alleyways going up and going down, and intersected here and there by steps of grey stone; and because there is no traffic in a town located at this height, the tiny pointed paving stones are all covered with spindly grass of a yellowish-green hue.

Doors that lead to vast cellars below street level where whole poverty-stricken families live in age-old dankness.

Shops with small, coloured window displays; Oriental boutiques, narrow and full of smoke where one can hear the drawl of nasal voices ...

Here and there a young man leans against a wall and makes signs to a girl bending over the railing of her balcony ...

Peasants wearing headdresses that hang all the way down their black jackets pleated over their white calico trousers. Tanned and bearded figures with deep-set eyes, heavy eyebrows and fierce, wary faces, a strange mixture of Greek mountain-dwellers and of tribesmen.

There is an Arab beauty about the women. The expression in their large languorous and melancholy jet-black eyes is resigned and sad like that of wary animals.

Beggars whine obsequiously in their incessant pursuit of

3

the stranger everywhere he goes ... Songs that sound infinitely sad, refrains that are curiously gripping, just like those heard in Africa, a place one cannot help but long for.

Cagliari, Thursday 18 January, 5.30 p.m.

Ever since I have been here, memories of *La Villa Neuve*[4] haunt me more and more ... good ones and bad ones alike ... I say good ones, for now that all is dead and buried, I must not harbour any grudges against my poor hovel ... I must not forget that it did shelter Mummy and her sweet kind heart, Vava[5] and all his good intentions, none of which he ever carried out. Ever since I walked out of it, I have lived as if in a swift and dazzling reverie, moving through varied scenery under different names and guises.

I realise that the fairly restful winter I am spending here is but a breathing spell from the life that will be mine until the very end.

In a few days' time my aimless wanderings will take over again. Where? How? Only God can tell. I must not even speculate on that subject any longer, for just as I was about to stay on in Paris for months on end, I ended up in Cagliari of all places, an out-of-the-way spot if ever there was one.

Yet there is one thing to cheer me: the farther behind I leave the past, the closer I am to forging my own character. I am developing the most unflinching and invincible will, to say nothing of integrity, two traits I value more than any others and, alas, ones that are so hard to find in women.

That and the likely prospect of spending four months in the desert next spring make me feel confident of making a name for myself and, what's more, sooner or later fulfilling my life's goal.

I have given up the hope of ever having a corner on earth to call my own, a home, a family, peace or prosperity. I have donned the cloak of the rootless wanderer, one that can be a burden too at times. I have written off the thought of ever coming home to a happy family for rest and safety.

For the moment I have found a soothing enough temporary home here in Cagliari, and have the illusion of truly loving someone whose presence seems to have become a

4

must[6] ... Yet that dream too will be short-lived, for I shall need to be alone again and do without the tranquil indolence of a shared existence once the moment will have come again for rough and risky travel.

That is what must be, and so it shall be. And in the gloom of that future existence I shall at least have one consolation, the thought that upon my return a friend, a living being may be happy to see me again. What is so terrible though, is the length of time spent apart to make for such reunions ... And who knows, someone else may have taken my place by then. That is more than likely, given his ideas about women and marriage. It would be very strange indeed if he were never to meet a woman with whom to share those ideas which are so at odds with mine. I know that no such partner will appear while he is a vagabond outcast, unless he is prepared to make do with a wife somewhere who will quiver at the thought of him in danger, but only from a safe and comfortable distance.

But then he too, like Augustin, will yield to the lure of home and comfort once the present period of transition is behind him.

When that happens I will have no choice but to resume my journey, sad but certain of having nothing to look forward to but the empty hotel rooms, gourbis and tents that are the nomad's temporary shelter. ☽ Mektoub!

The only thing to do is take things as they come and enjoy this heady interlude, for it will soon be over.

Cagliari, 29 January 1900

My brief interlude in this ancient Sardinian town has now come to an end.

Tomorrow at this time I shall be quite far from these Cagliari cliffs, on that leaden, grumbling, turbulent sea.

Last night Cagliari was booming with the echo of its rolling thunder ... Today, the sea looks its most ominous; it has a dull shimmer.

I am full of the sorrow that goes with changes in surroundings, those successive stages of annihilation that slowly lead to the great and final void.

5

Isabelle travels to Paris and to Geneva in an attempt to sort out her inheritance.

Geneva, 27 May 1900, 9.30 p.m. [Sunday]

Back to this gloomy diary of mine in this evil city where I have suffered so much and have come close to perishing.

I have hardly been here a week and once again I feel as morbid and oppressed as I used to in the old days. All I want to do is get out for good.

I went to have a look at our poor house, with the sky low and sunless; the place was boarded up and mute, lost among the weeds.

I saw the road, white as ever, white like a silvery river heading for the Jura's great mountaintops between those tall velvet trees.

I saw the two graves in that faithless cemetery,[7] set in a land of exile so very far away from that other sacred place devoted to eternal repose and everlasting silence[8] ...

I feel that I have now become a total stranger on this soil which I shall leave tomorrow and hope never to visit again.

(Recorded later)
Paris, April 1900

In the misty light of stars and streetlamps one night I saw the Montparnasse cemetery's white crosses outlined like so many ghosts against the velvety black of big trees, and it occurred to me that the powerful rumble of Paris could not disturb the slumber of all the strangers lying there ...

JOURNAL TWO

*Journal Two is started in Geneva where Isabelle remains
for some time.*

In the name of God, the Merciful, the Compassionate!

Epitaph found on a grave in the little Vernier cemetery on 4
June 1899, the day I left Geneva and made a last pilgrimage to Vava's grave:
  *Peace to your ashes, to those that lie buried
  in that far-off foreign country, and to you who
  rest upon that sacred mound above the Mediterranean's
  eternal blue waves ...*

Geneva, 8 June 1900
*Upon my return from the Vernier cemetery. Feeling
infinitely sad.*

*So much travelling will put the mind to sleep; one gets used
to anything, whether to the most outstandingly exotic
places or the most remarkable faces. Yet there are times
when one suddenly wakes up and takes stock, only to be
suddenly struck by the strangeness of one's surroundings.*[9]

Over there in Africa, above the great blue gulf of unforgettable Annéba, stands the graveyard on the hill under the
blazing sky. The white marble tombs, and those made of
glazed, multi-coloured tiles must look like bright flowers
among the tall black cypresses and geraniums the colour of
blood or pale flesh, and fig trees from the Barbary Coast ...
  As I sat in the low grass of the Vernier graveyard facing
the two grey tombs set among the weeds of spring, I
thought of the grave of the † *White Spirit*[10] ... And in the

midst of all that indestructible Nature, my thoughts turned once again to the mystery of the end of people's lives ...

How useless and funereal are these notes of mine, and how despairingly monotonous, without even the slightest hint of gaiety or of hope.

The only consolation they contain is their growing sense of Islamic *resignation*. I would like it if Archivir[11] were to smile at me as only he can and if I were to hear him tell me in that tone of voice of his, the way he did the day I came so close to baring my soul: 'Go, Mahmoud, and do great, magnificent deeds ... Be a hero ...'

It is true that of all the men I have come across, this one, whose beloved picture I have in front of me, is the most spellbinding of all, and that his charm is of the most lofty and noble sort: he speaks to the soul rather than to the senses, he exalts whatever is sublime and stifles the low and contemptible. No one has ever had such a truly beneficial effect upon my soul. No one has ever understood and bolstered those blessed things that, since the ✝ *White Spirit*'s death, have slowly but surely begun to take root in my heart: faith, repentance, the desire for moral perfection, the longing for a reputation based on noble *merit*, and a thirst for great and magnificent deeds.

I judge and love him for what I have seen of him so far. Time will tell whether I have been clairvoyant, whether I have seen him as he really is, or whether I have made another mistake.

That will be the end of it once and for all, for if what I hold to be purity itself turns out to have a hidden blemish, if what looks to me like beauty masks the usual horror, if the light I take to be a beacon in life's black maze is a trick meant to lead wayfarers astray, what can I expect after that?

Yet once again, nothing, absolutely nothing has so far suggested there might be anything in such an unthinkable thought ... If he is the way I think he is, he may well put me through terrible paces, but in a magnificent way ... he may well turn out to be responsible for sending me off to die, but spare me the worst of grievances, namely disillusionment.

8

Thus said the Lord, Stand ye in the ways, and see, and ask for the old paths, where is the good way, and walk therein, and ye shall find rest for your souls. [JEREMIAH 6:16]

I shall always cherish the memory of these past few days spent in greater *happiness* and less *gloom*, for they are moments stolen from life's hopelessness, hours snatched from the void.

People who interest me are those who are subject to that lofty, fertile form of suffering known as dissatisfaction with oneself; the thirst for an 'Ideal', something mystical and eminently desirable that fires their souls ... Self-satisfaction because of some accomplishment will never be for me, and as I see it, truly superior people are those preoccupied with the quest for better selves.

Not for me are those who feel smug, happy with themselves and their lot, content with the state of their heart.

Not for me those solid citizens who are *deaf, dumb and blind and never admit a mistake.*

I must learn to *think*. That may be painful and take time.

I cannot describe the contempt and loathing I have for my own inadequacy, my obsessive need to see people however banal, to prostitute my soul and go into sickening explanations.

Instead of looking into myself for what my soul requires, why do I look in others, where I know it cannot be found?

Why can't I react against this impulse that continues to encumber my life? Except with very rare people, there is no such thing as communication on an intellectual plane, so why insist on courting disappointment?

LITERARY IDEAS

I think that, as a beginner, I must first of all develop the artistic side of my work, that is to say my *style*.

A symbol of what my life is now all about, and probably always will be, is that sign saying '*Room for rent*' by the window of the seedy room I am living in, with a camp bed in it, some papers and my handful of books.

Following a night of suffering, a strange morning ...

I realise that I cannot write right now.

I shall confine myself to describing the situation: a purely cerebral wish to improve my conduct and get to work ... no enthusiasm, though, for either.

I am suddenly aware of my growing resolve to set off for Ouargla at any cost, and try once more to isolate myself for months on end in the total silence of the Desert and get used to that slow dreamy life out there.[12]

Nothing is standing in my way, come to think of it.

However limited my means, I will still be able to afford to live there as well as it is wise to live.

Oddly enough, I have not forgotten all that I went through down there, the unbelievable hardships, my illness...

They must have been due to unfortunate circumstances though, and the whole idea now appeals to me a lot.

This time around, life in the Desert will be a bit less exhausting as I will not have to stay up all night, but it will complete my education as a man of action, the Spartan education I need.

What bitter ecstasies await me: first the farewell to that strange man Archivir who has given me such a remarkable time, sweet and bitter all at once.

Next, there will be the solemn occasion of my boarding ship at Marseilles and saying goodbye to the brother who is the apple of my eye ...

Then there will be the sad but soothing moment of my pilgrimage to Annéba, to her grave on that hallowed hillside.

Then on to Batna, where I left behind so many nostalgic memories ...

Torrid Biskra, where I used to spend such charming evenings in front of the Moorish cafés ...

And that steep and blistering road to arid Oued Rir ...

And what about sad Tuggurt sleeping underneath its shroud of salt as it overlooks its hidden shott ...

And finally Ouargla, the very gateway to that mysterious

10

void known as the great Sahara, which so appeals to my imagination ...

I would like to go to Ouargla, settle there and *make a home, something I miss more and more.* A little mud house close to some date palms, a place to cultivate the odd vegetable in the oasis, a servant and companion, a few small animals to warm my lonely heart, a horse perhaps, and books as well.

Lead two lives, one that is full of adventure and belongs to the Desert, and one, calm and restful, devoted to thought and far from all that might interfere with it.

I should also want to travel now and then, to visit Augustin, and go to Paris, only to return to my solitary, silent retreat.

Fashion a soul for myself out there, an awareness, an intelligence and a will.

I have no doubt that my attraction to the Islamic faith would blossom magnificently over there.

Should anyone happen to take the trouble to read this diary one day, it would be a faithful mirror of the fast pace of my life which, for all I know, may already be in its final stages.

After two days of dreadful boredom, I am trying to get back to work.

I feel more and more disgusted with my second self, that no-good oaf who rears his head from time to time, usually, if not always, under the influence of physical factors. Better health, in other words, would clearly result in an improvement in the intellectual and spiritual side of my life.

Night before last I had a long discussion with Archivir about that perennial subject of ours, namely pleasure. I still hold on to my theory, which says that one should limit one's needs as much as one can to avoid disillusionment, as well as to avoid any dulling of the senses owing to unpleasant sensations.

Archivir, on the other hand, maintains that needs must be developed, and that one must use one's last ounce of energy to satisfy them.

It occurs to me this instant to write a dissertation on the subject, to be published perhaps in *L'Athénée*.

Once again, I feel that I am going through a period of intellectual incubation which I think will be the most fertile of my whole life so far.

Reading the *Journal des Goncourts* does me a great deal of good. I shall have to use my stay in Marseilles to read the other volumes and make notes.

I have so far opted for reading matter which focuses on feelings and on the imagination. As a result, my sense of poetry has been overdeveloped at the expense of rigorous thought.

The *Journal des Goncourts* is a work that forces one to think, and *deeply* so. I must look for other, similar books and use them for discussion and debate, while I am still surrounded by people.

I am clearly aware that certain things I do are absolutely *futile, stupid* and *actually bad* for my future; is my will not strong enough to stand up to my ego and prevent these things?

A matter to be studied, so that I can find out how to do better.

'*We now have only one main interest in life: the gratification that comes from observing reality. Without that, life is boring and empty*'.[13]

Written 30 June, 8 o'clock in the evening

The more I write and develop my story, the more I feel curiously *bored* with it, hence those nagging doubts about what possible interest it may have for the reader.

It is therefore no exaggeration to say that I can no longer make up my mind whether *Rakhil*[14] is or is not a sickening pile of badly written police reports.

That is why I need to read it out loud to someone. Needless to say, if the book makes the same impression on readers as it does on me, then no one will read beyond the second page after the foreword.

Everything seems so tranquil this evening, despite the noise coming from the boulevards that teem with people. Everything is in a soft grey fog, just like my mood: I am not feeling overly emotional, but feel no enthusiasm either. All I want to do is work in peace and develop what intelligence I have.

Such apparent egocentricity to be found on every page of this diary should not be taken for megalomania ... Oh, no ... To begin with, loners are given to constant introspection; and I do need to compile a record that will give me, later on, a true image of my soul as it is today. That is the only way I shall be able to judge my present life and to see whether my character has progressed or not.

Written at Geneva, 3 July, 1900, 11.30 at night

I am thinking of writing a short story, to go with *La Voie*,[15] but with very different characters: Semenov, Andreyev, Sacha in Paris.

The same night, at 2 in the morning

I am not asleep. I don't feel like it in the least. Downstairs I can hear the piercing screams of a Russian woman in labour. What an ominous way of entering into the world, on such a rainy night, ominous and *symbolic* as well.

The first thing we do in life is weep ... And how much our entrance resembles our exit, except that our exit is less sad than our entrance, with all the woes that it entails!

Weep ye not for the dead, neither bemoan him; but weep sore for him that goeth away: for he shall return no more nor see his native country. (JEREMIAH, 22:10)

Isabelle leaves Geneva for Marseilles, where Augustin and his wife have now set up their meagre household.

Departure from Geneva, 14 July 1900, 7.30 p.m.
The weather is grey and stormy and dark. Where am I going? ... ☽ *Where Destiny is taking me!*

13

Arrival in Marseilles. Fatigue. Superb sunrise over the Crau.

A sense of Africa. My voyage has gone well.

An idea occurs to me as I come upon the following phrase in the *Journal des Goncourts*: 'finished *Manette Salomon* today.' No work of literature is ever finished in the sense that it cannot bear improvement. To finish something is to feel satisfied with it.

Despite the chaos and my disgust those last few days in Geneva, that month of living the Russian way – for the last time in my life no doubt – will always be one of my most cherished memories.

My brief romance with Archivir also had its considerable charm, yet I have said goodbye to him for ever, without hard feelings of any sort.

The phenomenon of malice in the domain of love, whether such malice is physical or mental, is a sure sign that civilisation is on the wane.[16]

I would still like to make a stab at happiness, in the form of a solitary nest for myself in some far-off place where I can be independent.

That is the kind of nest I am going to try to build for myself in the middle of the Desert, far away from people. I want to be alone for months on end, without any human contact whatsoever. I must avoid sharing anyone's lot from now on, whether in embarrassing love affairs or in friendships.[17]

That will at least spare me a good deal of suffering.

I must also try to create for myself an inner world of thoughts and feelings, to compensate for my solitude and poverty.[18]

However difficult, I must live out my theory of limiting one's needs.

14

That will not be hard to do, as long as my health holds out.

Out there, I shall be able to have a hygienic sort of life if I lead a reasonably settled existence. That way I shall be able to avoid the roots of ill health.

As for my state of mind, it has now become more than urgent that I get down to work.

That would not only ensure me a chance to earn a living now that my feeble means have been wiped out but would also safeguard me against my usual despondency.

I must learn to live in the *present moment* and not in the future only. While to live in the past and think of what was good and beautiful about it amounts to a sort of *seasoning* of the present, the perennial wait for tomorrow is bound to result in chronic discontent that poisons one's entire outlook.

I must learn to feel *more deeply*, to see *better*, and above all, to *think*.

18 July 1900, 9 p.m.

It does look as though things have been decided at last, as though I am actually off to Africa on Saturday, after an absence of nine months. My God, if only upon reaching Ouargla I could muster the courage to set up the nest I need so much, and stay there for at least six months, I could do some *work*.

Tonight I will re-read the whole of my novel *Rakhil*. In order to discover what I think of it, I need the one thing I have not had — an overall view. All it now needs to stand as a story is the scene with the Jewish women going for a stroll, which would amount to a half hour's work. Before I do anything else, however, I must finish reading and annotating the *Journal des Goncourts* while I am still here.

Next, I must take note of the odd passage from other writers: Baudelaire, Zola, Loti.

While travelling, I must carefully write down not only *factual information*, but also my *impressions*. I must come up with an interesting and picturesque description of my crossing of the Mediterranean and my journey through the ancient sites of Algeria and the Oued Rir. That will be the first thing to put down on paper there.

I must also write down everything I see in the oasis; a detailed summary with as much information as possible. After that, I shall start a *literary diary* about my life out there. Meanwhile, I must try to turn my book *Rakhil* into what it has got to be above all else – a true work of art.

I must also, for publication in Russian, write a description of my journey through the Sahel last autumn, plus a few † short stories.

A gruelling workload, but it is my only road to salvation. Then, once I have *La Villa Neuve* out of the way, I shall go to Paris, if I can afford it, to lead an altogether different life than I did before. I shall do everything within my power to make a success of the material I bring along.[19]

That is the only sensible plan I can make for the moment.

If by autumn there is a move toward Morocco, I will of course go along and take detailed notes at all times.

Yesterday, 17 July, at four in the afternoon, I took the omnibus down the Cours Devilliers to the Quai de la Fraternité. I thought Marseilles looked very colourful, true to form.

I went for a long walk with Augustin, and we first stopped at the Fort Saint-Nicolas bridge. We watched the exertion necessary to turn the bridge around and let through a Greek sailboat named *Eleni*. At the bow stood a man with a coarse face, in shirtsleeves and a felt hat, who kept shouting: *Vira, vira, vira!* to the crew trying to steer the vessel.

Silhouettes of young bathers in their bathing trunks, who looked happy to be wet and naked in the sun and kept striking poses.

We crossed the old harbour by ferry below Fort Saint-Jean and paid a visit to the Quai de la Joliette, across from the Africa-bound ships.

Huge black heaps, black dust and black-looking men in rags and covered with soot; the whites of their eyes looked dirty, their mouths looked like wounds and any patch of real skin that showed through might as well have been the hideous mark of leprosy. Equally black tavern, where a sunburnt man with the face of a crook was having an

16

argument with a frightened coaldocker. Back to the jetty. The horizon looked a greenish aquamarine and the sea was slightly choppy. Watched a net being pulled in between two heaving boats.

Quai du Lazaret. Back in the coal tavern, a man had asked me for a light and, already very drunk, had kept singing and making a lot of noise. We saw him again on the quay, sitting on top of his cart, waving, holding forth and laughing in the midst of a crowd, under the gaze and indulgent smiles of the police who were probably biding their time to arrest him ... something about the drunkard having crushed a soldier's leg.

We came home at eight o'clock. Fatigue, intense head-ache and nausea.

Friday 20 July 10 p.m.
in Marseilles

Everything is finished, packed and closed ... The only thing left here is my camp bed, which must wait till morning.

At one in the afternoon tomorrow I leave for Algiers.

The fact is that I did not really quite believe I would actually be leaving for Ouargla. So many things had stood in the way of my carrying out my daring plan.

My chances of success are good, for I leave well equipped. As for my mood, I feel great sadness, as I now do every time I leave this house, even though I am no more than a passing stranger in it.

Yet I also feel a glimmer of hope. I know my present mood will pass as soon as I am with my friend Eugène[20] in Algiers, when there will be new impressions for me to take in.

In any event I must work, and write, over there ... My God, if I could only muster the energy to buckle down and finish part at least of all I have got to do! Would it not be a better idea to start my description of my trip through Algeria with Bône rather than Algiers? If I came across any impressions that warrant recording, I could present them as recollections from another period. That would give me the opportunity to produce some splendidly melancholy pages, in the vein of African perspectives.

17

That trip will give me the material for a book, a good one I can write quickly and that can perhaps be published before *Rakhil*.

I sometimes feel so pessimistic I look at the future with a feeling of irrational terror, as if it can only be bad and terrifying, even though many of those dark clouds have in fact gone from my horizon.

Isabelle quits Marseilles and returns to North Africa, arriving in Algiers on 22 July.

Algiers, 22 July 1900, 11 p.m.

It was hot yesterday afternoon when I boarded the same ship I took last September.[21] I kept staring at Augustin's silhouette till it disappeared from view when the ship tacked. I then studied the view. The harbour was full of the powerful red and black shapes of transatlantic steamers.

Then came the city ... to begin with, when the ship was in the middle of the harbour, Marseilles looked like a delicate palette of grisailles: the grey of the smoky sky, the blue tones of the mountains, the pinkish-grey ones of the rooftops ... the lilac hues of the sea, while the hardy vegetation growing among the rocks provided so many dots of a greenish-brown ... The green foliage of the plane trees, the cathedral's gilded cupolas and statue of the Virgin Mary were the only things to stand out in sharp and lively contrast.

Yet once the ship was at some distance, everything looked quite different: it was all a monochrome gold, so intense one could hardly believe one's eyes.

Spent a peaceful night on the sternside bench. Felt truly well; woke up by about 2.45 a.m.

Saw the sun come up while sailors were putting up the canvas. First there was a rosy dawn, then a crimson disc appeared, clear-cut in outline. Slightly above it were the lacy shapes of pink clouds outlined in gold.

All night long I had the feeling of mysterious well-being I always get when peacefully asleep with the ship's lights shining over my head.

I will continue this report tomorrow.

18

Oh, the sense of bliss I had this evening, knowing that I am *back* inside solemn mosques and in the ancient hustle and bustle of the Arab quarter in the Rue Jénina!

Oh that extraordinary feeling of intoxication I had tonight, in the peaceful shadows of the great al-Jadid Mosque during the icha prayer!

I feel I am coming back to life again ... ☽ *Lead us along the straight path, the one taken by those to whom you have been generous!*

For a long, long time all you could see of the Algerian coast was Matifou steeped in vapours ...

Next one could see the Algiers triangle, with the old part of town looking like an avalanche of snow ... this was followed by a splendid view of the entire panorama in full daylight.

After a very brief moment spent in my room with Eugène, he left and I went exploring by myself. My hat bothered me, though, for it set me apart from Muslims.

I went back to don my fez, and went out again with Ahmed, the manservant, to go to the al-Kabir Mosque. It was so cool and peaceful there underneath those white arcades. Went to greet the mosque's wakil, a venerable old man who sat in a side niche writing on his knee.

Nothing surprises him any longer. No undue curiosity, no indiscretion. I then went to that charming blue-tinted zawyia of Sidi-Abd-al-Rahman.

Stood for a while in the cool shade facing the mihrab upon those thick rugs. Drank some jasmine-flavoured water from the earthenware pitcher on the windowsill.

The zawyia is one of great beauty, and I will certainly go back there before I leave Algiers.

Dashes of an unvarnished bluish-white among the greenery in the Jardin Marengo.

Smelled a sweet and heady fragrance I could not place as I walked through it, of flowers I could not identify.

Had supper at Al-Haj-Muhammad, on the corner of the Rue Jénina. Felt *intensely* happy to be here again, on this African soil to which I feel tied not only by memories but also by that strange appeal it has always had for me, even before I had ever seen it, when I was still living in that boring *Villa* of ours.

I felt so happy sitting at that table, a feeling impossible to describe, one I have never felt anywhere but in Africa.

How much Arabs resemble each other!

At Haj-Muhammad's yesterday I saw men come in whom I thought I had known in earlier days, in Bône, Batna, or in the South ... but not in Tunisia, where they look very different.

After dinner this evening, went to say the icha prayer in the al-Jadid Mosque which is less beautiful than the two others, but the soaring sense of Islam was superb.

The place was cool and dark as I went in, and a handful of oil-lamps were the only source of light.

A feeling of ancient Islam, tranquil and mysterious.

Stood for a long time near the mihrab. Somewhere far behind us a clear, high voice went up, a dreamlike voice that took turns with that of the elderly Imam standing in the mihrab where he recited the *fatiha*.

Standing next to each other, we all prayed as we listened to the exhilarating yet solemn exchange between those two voices. The one in front of us sounded old and hoarse, but gradually grew louder and louder till it was strong and powerful, while the other one seemed to come from somewhere high up in the mosque's dark reaches as it sang triumphantly in regular intervals of its unshakable, radiant faith in Allah and His Prophet ... I was in ecstasy as my heart soared up towards the celestial sphere from whence the second voice poured forth in sweet and confident bliss.

Oh, to lie upon the rugs of some silent mosque, far from the noise of wanton city life, and, eyes closed, gaze turned heavenwards, listen to Islam's song for ever!

I remember the time I wandered around till daybreak one night last year. I ended up by the Morkad ruins at the foot of the minaret, where the windows were all lit up. In the dead silence of the night I heard the muezzin's voice, which sounded infinitely mysterious as it sang ☽ *Prayer is better than sleep!* Those rhythmical notes still echo in my ears.

20

After the icha prayer, which is a lovely moment of the day, I went out for an aimless stroll.

Upon my return around ten o'clock, I spent some time in front of a small shop in a narrow street. The place was lit by an oil lamp. A guitar, pipestems and decoration in the form of paper cutouts.

The shopkeeper was stretched out on an oval mat in front, a dark, handsome indifferent-looking man whose gestures were very slow, as though his mind were elsewhere. Might that have been due to kif?

Bought a small pipe and some kif.

That more or less sums up what I did yesterday.

The day of my arrival has turned out to be an incomparably happy one.

Isabelle now begins her journey southward to the Souf region, where she sets up house in El Oued.

El-Merayer, 30 July 1900

Left Algiers on 27 July, eight o'clock in the morning.

Frame of mind fairly good, but spoiled by the presence of Lieutenant Lagrange's mistress, a horrible revolting creature.

At Sidi-Amram, I lay down near some burning dried djerid, next to a French soldier who had turned up out of the blue; drank some coffee, felt weak, slightly feverish. The fire's flames cast a strange red light upon the mud walls, underneath the stars.

Tuggurt, 31 July 1900, Tuesday noon

I am sitting in the obscurity of the dining room, to get away from the innumerable flies in my own room.

I am pleased to see the desert's torrid heat does not bother me too much, even though I am not feeling altogether normal because I am worn out by my journey and recent late nights. I can work and think. In fact, it is only today that I am beginning to recover. I will not really feel well, though, until the day I have settled in El Oued and all is quiet around me.

21

I am also beginning to find out about thrift and the willpower it takes to avoid squandering the little money I have left.

I must also remember that I have come to the desert, not to indulge in last year's dolce far niente, but to work, and that this journey of mine can either mean disaster for the rest of my life, or prove a prelude to salvation for both body and soul, depending on how well I manage.

I have an altogether charming memory of Algiers, from the first night to the last in particular.

The last evening I went with Mokhtar and Abd-el-Kaim Oulid-Issa to a tobacconist's on the Plateau Saulières. We had a rather lively conversation, and then went for a melancholy stroll along the quays. Ben Elimaur, Mokhtar and Zarrouk, the medical student, softly sang wistful Algerian songs.

I had several moments of great and altogether Oriental intensity at Algiers.

The long journey I made in third class, alone with someone as young as Mokhtar, also had its charm.

I have said farewell to the big Blue Sea, perhaps for a long time to come.

I travelled through wild Kabyle territory and a landscape of jagged rocks. Then, after the hills of the Portes de Fer, came the desolate plateaux gilded by fields cultivated by Arabs – long dots of a tawny-silvery hue upon the landscape's oranges and ochres.

The plains at Borj-bou-Arérij offer a desperately sad and dreary spectacle.

Saint Arnaud is a large village lost among the high plateaux of Cheonïya country. Yet Saint Arnaud, *Elelma* in Arabic, is a verdant spot. Its gardens are like those of the Randon column at Bône.

The Cadi is a noble and serene old man, who belongs to another age.

In ten, twenty years' time, will today's young Algerians resemble their fathers and be as steeped as they are in the solemn serenity of their Islamic faith? His son Si Ali seems at first sight to be sleepy and heavy. Yet he is an intelligent man who does care about the public interest. Si Ihsan, who is of Turkish origin, is a man whose charm lies in his candour.

Had an intense and ever so pleasant sense of old Africa and Bedouin country the first night at Elelma: there was the distant sound of dogs barking all night long, and the crowing of the rooster.

Crossed the Ourlana oasis around two in the morning last night: vast gardens enclosed by walls made of clay, segniyas reeking of saltpetre, humidity and fever.

The houses built of ochre-coloured mud all seemed to be in a state of slumber.

At Sidi Amram I stretched out on the ground by a fire that was burning dried djerids. The sand felt warm and the sky was ablaze with countless stars.[22]

Oh Sahara, Sahara so full of perils, you hide your soul in bleak inhospitable solitudes!

I love this country of sand and stone, inhabited by camels and primitive men, and dotted with treacherous shotts and sebhkas.

Between Mraïer and El Berd last night I saw bizarre, fetishistic forms garbed in red and white rags, at the exact spot where a Muslim was assassinated a few years ago. It is a forlorn monument put up in memory of the man who lies buried at Tuggurt.

Borj Terjen, 1 August, 7 a.m.

Set off from Taïbet at 4.45 yesterday afternoon on N'Tardjallah's mule with Muhammad al-Haj. Reached Mguetla by nine o'clock.

In spite of slight fatigue, had excellent impression of first encampment.

A wind that was almost cold during the night, and in the dunes a murmur like that of the sea. A feeling of desolation, for no reason at all.

Magnificent sunrise. Arose at 4 a.m. A pristine sky, cool and rather strong north-easterly wind.

Set off at five o'clock. Struck camp and made coffee in the dunes. The mailcoach caught up with us. Rode a camel till Terjen. Arrived at eight.

Excellent frame of mind. State of health, *ditto*.

How wise I have been to leave Europe and decide to make my home in El Oued, which is what I did yesterday.

Provided my health holds up, I must stay at El Oued as long as I can.

Above all, I hope this is not a waste of time, especially vis à vis my intellectual and spiritual development and my literary endeavours. ☽ *Please Allah!*

El Oued, 4 August 1900, 7 a.m.

As I finished writing in my diary at Terjen, I sat down on my bed, facing the door.

Had an indescribable sense of well-being and profound bliss at being there ... Siesta interrupted by children and goats.

Left with the mailcoach around 2.30 p.m. Intense heat. Did not feel well. Mounted the camel once more. Reached Mouïet-el-Caïd by maghreb [6 p.m.].

By 4 a.m. off to Ourmes, where we arrived by half-past seven. Crossed the biggest dune and came upon several dead camels, one of which was a recent casualty.

Ourmes. Siesta in the park. An enchanted sight. Did not sleep well because of inevitable flies and hot burnous. Was at El Oued around maghreb.

Went to see a house that belongs to a Caïd, on the town square opposite the Borj. Rented it. Have started moving in.

The evening of my arrival, beautiful ride on mules. A night that looked transparent on the white sand. A deep garden, fast asleep in darkness. Nothing but things cool and mellow all around.

Have now reached my goal at long last; now I must get to work with all the energy I can muster. As soon as I receive the money from Eugène, I must pay the rent, Habib, and buy basic necessities.

My luggage is to arrive today. As soon as I am living in less of a makeshift situation, I shall have to start writing the book about my journey, the first chapter of which will deal with Marseilles.

I am far from society, far from civilisation. I am by myself, on Muslim soil, out in the desert, free and in the best of circumstances, except for my health and even that is not too bad. The outcome of my undertaking is therefore up to me ...

I am beginning to feel bored, for my luggage has not turned up and I cannot get on with my house and life ...

Habib's house. A square building of unbleached toub, in one of the winding streets paved with fine sand, not far from the dune.

Off in a corner is a small dark goat with an amulet around its neck. Habib's many brothers come and go. The old man's wife, tall and slim, dressed in long white veils, a veritable mountain on top of her head: braids of black hair, braids and tassels made of red wool, and in her ears heavy iron rings held up by cords tied to the hairdo. To go out, she throws a blue veil over it all. A strange, ageless figure with a sunburnt skin and doleful black eyes.

Temperatures will soon start going down. There is already a little gust of wind from time to time.

To sum things up, I have not yet embarked upon my new way of life. Too much of it is still unsettled.

El Oued, Thursday 9 August 7.30 p.m.

For the time being there is nothing durable about this Arab lifestyle of mine, which is indolent but in no way dangerous for I know it will not last. My little household is beginning to look like one. I am still short of money though.

I must avoid borrowing any from the bach-adel, for he is clearly no altruist.

A few days from now I expect to change my lifestyle altogether.

Every evening we go to Bir Arby. We go across the snow-white sands translucent in the moonlight. We pass the gloomy-looking silhouettes of the Christian cemetery: high grey walls with a black cross on top ... The impression is a lugubrious one. From there we go up a low hill, and in a deep and narrow valley we see the garden, which is no different from any other Souafa garden. At the bottom stand the highest palm trees, the smaller ones grow near the wells.

In the bluish-green light of the moon they look diaphanous, like delicate feathery plumes. Between their handsome chiselled trunks lies the odd verdant stretch of melons, water-melons and fragrant basil.

The water is clear and cool. The well's primitive iron frame made a squeaking noise and the goatskin fell in and made lapping noises in the well's dark interior before surfacing again, dripping wet. I threw my chechiya down on the sand, soaked my head in the oumara and took a few greedy gulps of water. It was refreshing and cool, and gave me the sort of shiver that a drink of water always does down here. After that we stretched out on the sand for a moment.

Slowly and laboriously, we headed back for the sleeping town and that white house that is now my home, God knows for how long ...

Isabelle meets Slimène Ehnni, and begins to frequent the Kadrya confraternity to which he belongs.

A few nights ago I spent a night in a large garden that belongs to the Hacheich Caidat, west of El Oued, together with Slimène.[23]

Not a soul was breathing in the palm trees' shadows. We sat down near a well where I had unsuccessfully tried to draw water with a torn oumara. We both felt sad, in my case because of the trouble owing to local indiscretions which loomed large in my mind.

My soul has aged, alas. It has ceased to delude itself and I can only smile at Slimène's dreams. He does not believe in eternity but thinks that earthly love goes on for ever. He also wonders what will happen in a year's, in seven years' time.[24]

Yet what would be the use of telling him, of making him sad and hurting him. That will happen soon enough, the day we go our separate ways.

After an hour spent talking, with tears in our eyes, about the truly awful possibilities ahead, we went to sleep under the palm trees on top of our burnous, using a thickness of sand for a pillow.

Slept till about 2.30 a.m. In the rising pre-dawn chill, we laboriously retraced our steps up the path through the dunes. A maze of tiny alleyways reeking heavily of salt-

26

petre, rather like the Oued Rir oases. Crossed the market-place which was deserted except for a few camels and their drivers, asleep by the great well's iron frame.

Rode the bad white horse last night, taking the road to Kouïnine through El Oued's tiny suburbs, where black and white goats graze on top of the roofs of zéribas made of djérid.

To the west, in the direction of Kouïnine and Tuggurt, the sun was a ball of blood sinking in a blaze of gold and crimson. The slopes of the dunes seemed to be on fire below the ridges, in hues that deepened from one moment to the next.

This morning the sky looked dark and cloudy, a most unexpected sight in this land of implacably blue skies and perennial sunshine.

The fact is that at the moment my time is not being put to good use. The siesta hour has a lot to do with that.

I would like to start working. That would mean getting up for reveille, at the very least, and not going back to bed after Slimène has left ... I do, alas, from sheer boredom and from the fact that I have nothing else to do.

I must go out right after reveille, for the occasional morning ride, on whatever horse happens to be available.

Spent a quarter of an hour taking measures against the swarms of flies in my two rooms. The day will come when I will cherish the memory of such tiny chores in this very simple lifestyle of mine.

Oh, if my present way of life could last, if Slimène could continue to be the good friend and brother he is right now. And if only I could share more in the local side of life and get to work as soon as the weather starts to cool!

When a girl gets married over here she is taken to her husband on a man's back. To see his wife, the husband must hide for seven nights, come after the maghreb and leave before the morning.

Obviously a vestige of the abductions of earlier days.

18 August 1900, 3.30 p.m.

Went riding by myself last night, through the little town-ships all along the road to Tuggurt. Went through Teksebet.

27

A melancholy, derelict-looking place, virtually deserted, where ruins crumble with every step.

Headed back for El Oued by sundown. Watched the sand pour down the greyish dunes in a constant stream.

Getting in the saddle yesterday I heard nearby wails, the Arab way of broadcasting someone's death. The daughter of Salah the Spahi, young Abd-el-Kader's sister, had died.

The little girl was buried in the hot sand yesterday at maghreb ... she was swallowed up for all time by eternal night, like one of those meteors one sees flashing through this land's infinite sky.

Isabelle travels around the area on her horse 'Souf', named after the region.

Monday 9 October 1900, 9 a.m.

Shortly after the maghreb last night, rode Souf by the back of the café through the white sandy streets along houses that are half in ruin.

A few moments earlier, just as the sun had been about to set and El Oued had been ablaze in gold, I had spotted the silhouettes of two Arabs garbed in white standing on top of the little dune where the lime kiln is; they looked as if set against a heavenly light. The impression was a biblical one, and I suddenly felt as if transported back to the ancient days of primitive humanity, when the great light-giving bodies in the sky had been the object of veneration ...

At that frontier between town and desert, I was reminded of those autumn and winter sunsets in the land of exile, when the great snow-capped Jura mountains seemed to come closer in an expanse of pale bluish hues.

It is chilly in the morning now. The light has changed colour. We no longer have the flat glare of stifling summer days. The sky is now a violent shade of blue, pure and invigorating.

Everything has come to life again, and so has my soul. Yet, as always, I feel a boundless sadness, an inarticulate longing for something I cannot describe, a nostalgia for a *place* for which I have no name.

For several days now, intellectual endeavour has seemed

28

less repellent to me than it did this summer, and I think I shall go on writing. The wellspring does not seem to have run dry.

For the moment I do not feel up to taking off and parting from Slimène for ever, even if I could afford to do so. And why should I?

I feel a tranquil heart is mine at last; the same cannot be said for any peace of mind, alas!

Isabelle gets to know the two sons of the Grand Sheikh of the Kadrya, Sidi-el-Hussein and Si Lachmi.

El Oued, 27 October 1900, 9 p.m.

Went to Amiche on the 17th, to look for Sidi-el-Hussein.[25]

It was chilly when we left around six that morning. Arrived in no time at all at Sheikh Blanc's great zawyia, which seemed quite deserted, near those vast and gloomy cemeteries. Set off again with two menservants, and passed houses and gardens which looked quite picturesque.

Found Sidi-el-Hussein at long last at the far end of Ras-el-Amiche, facing the infinite stretches of sand that lead to the distant Sudan.

Spent the siesta hour with the sheikh in a narrow primitive room with no windows. It was vaulted and had sand on the floor, and it constituted the whole interior of the house, which stands all by itself.[26]

A strange figure showed up, an almost black Southerner with burning eyes who suffers from a form of epilepsy that makes him strike at anyone who touches or frightens him ... Yet he is also very congenial. Left at about three o'clock with the sheikh for the Chaambas colony. Set off again by myself around 3.15. Reached the cemeteries located to the right of Amiche by sundown. At the maghreb hour, stopped on the dune that overlooks the Ouled-Touati.

On my left the plains looked pink, and in the village I saw a few women in blue rags and an oddly shaped red dromedary. Utter peace and silence all around ... Came back home around 5.15 p.m.

I have now reached a state of destitution foreseen for some time. Yet, in bringing me to El Oued, Providence seems to have wanted to spare me worse suffering in other places.

Who knows, it may be that all these strokes of bad luck will merely serve to forge my character and pull me out of the indolent *indifference* that often comes over me when the future is at stake.

May God help me succeed! So far I have always survived even the worst and most perilous of pitfalls unscathed. Fate will not quite forsake me just yet, perhaps. ✝ *The ways of the Lord are inscrutable.*

4 November 1900

Took Souf this morning to go into the dunes and gardens that lie between the road to Tuggurt and the one that goes to Debila. Steep paths leading to the dunetops overlooking deep gardens down below.

It rained last night; the sand was wet and yellowish in colour, and gave off a nice and cool, slightly salty smell.

On the monotonous-looking hillsides grows the odd succulent, a light green and spindly sort of sedum. In the gardens the carrots and peppers look like bright green carpets.

My life remains the same, monotonous and devoid of real changes. It has even become very sheltered, for I spend part of my time inside my house (which I consider as no more than temporary quarters as we are about to move) and part in Mansour's place. Often I go to the house of Abd-el-Kader, of whom I am growing truly fond. If I could come up with the odd book in his place, I would feel very gratified indeed.

As for Slimène, nothing has changed, and I grow more attached to him by the day, for he is truly turning into a member of my family, or rather *all the family I have got* ... May that last for ever, even over here among these perennially grey sands ...!

I occasionally stand still and marvel at my astounding destiny ...

In an oasis somewhere in the desert, after all those grandiose dreams of mine!

And how will it all end?

El Oued, 1 December 1900
At the house of Salah ben Taliba

This December bears a curious resemblance to that of the disastrous year 1897. Same weather, same violent gusts of wind lashing against my face. In those days, I had the Mediterranean for a horizon, and I was still so young; even though recently bereaved I still had a full measure of *joie-de-vivre*.

I could never be content with the genteel pleasures of city life in Europe. The idea I had of heading for the desert to satisfy my strange need for both adventure and peace did require courage, but it was feasible and, as it turns out, inspired. As for domestic bliss, I have found it, and it seems to grow stronger day by day.

The only thing to threaten it is politics ... but alas! ☾ *Allah knows what is hidden in the heavens and on earth!* and no one can foretell the future.

Barely two weeks ago tonight I went to meet my *beloved* as far as the area south of Kouïnine.

I rode Souf in a darkness so grey it made my head spin.

Lost my way several times. Had strange impressions down in those plains, where the horizon seems to rise in the shape of dunes, and villages look like hedges made of djérid.

Was thinking about the passage in *Aziyadé* about Istanbul graves lit by dim and solitary lights, when I suddenly spotted the gate to the Teksebet cemetery's dome.

Poignant memories of the end of the ✝ *White Spirit*'s life have come to haunt me these last few days.

El Oued, Friday 14 December 1900, 2 p.m.

I am going to have a hard time getting through the winter without heat or money, for I am not at all able to leave this place.

I sat in the courtyard of the Elakbab Zawyia the other day, and marvelled at the strange scene I saw there: unusual-looking heads, those of sunburnt Chaambas from Troud in the South, half-covered in grey veils: the expres-

31

sion on their almost black faces was so spirited they looked ferocious ... in the dilapidated courtyard of the zawyia they all gravitated around that huge red-haired sheikh with his soft blue eyes[27] ...

My best memory of the South will no doubt be of that memorable day, the 3rd of December, when I had the good fortune to witness a breathtaking sight, the return of the great marabout Si Mahmoud Lachmi, a fascinating figure impossible to describe, whose strange personality had attracted me in Tuggurt. Si Lachmi is meant to have a strange hold over adventurous souls. On that winter morning, it was a heady experience to be engulfed by gunpowder, wild strains of music coming from the nefsaoua des bendar, frenetic shouts from the crowd welcoming one of the Prophet's descendants, and the frantic horses in the midst of all that smoke and uproar ...

24 December 1900 [Ramadan]

I have been feeling ill and weak, have had to cope with the side-effects of fasting, to say nothing of the far more serious matter of my financial problems, yet these Ramadan nights and mornings have quite unexpectedly brought me moments of a quiet and pleasurable serenity that borders on joy.

I see clearly now that the only way to lead a quiet life – which is not to say a happy one, for illness, misery and death exist – is to turn one's back on mankind with the exception of a tiny handful of chosen ones, still making sure one does not depend on them in any way.

Arab society as one finds it in the big cities, unhinged and vitiated as it is by its contact with a foreign world, does not exist down here. As for French civilisation ... from what I have been able to glean from the Infantry Lieutenant and especially the doctor, it has certainly gone downhill here.

Slimène is transferred to Batna; they must try to meet their debts.

28 January 1901, 8 a.m.

Once again, all has been shattered and destroyed: my indolent way of life has come to an abrupt end! No

32

more of the blissful serenity we had both begun to take for granted.

On the evening of the 23rd we found out by chance that Slimène was about to be relieved of his duties and sent back to Batna. It was a moment of unspeakable anguish and of near-despair ...

Nor was that all. To add to our sorrow at the thought of imminent departure and the hardships of life in Batna was our distress over our financial situation, and the hundred francs' worth of debts, which we could not even begin to pay.

A gloomy, sleepless night, spent drinking and smoking kif.

The next morning, a quick and worried visit to Sidi Lachmi. Found him surrounded by pilgrims about to leave for the sheikh of Nefta's great Ziara. Spent over an hour making small talk, while my mind was elsewhere and I had a lump in my throat. In the end I took the sheikh aside and agreed to come back with Slimène after the maghreb hour. I felt limp with exhaustion as I went home full trot, standing in the stirrups.

Found Slimène in a half-demented state, looking haggard and no longer aware of what he was doing. Went out on Souf that night shortly before maghreb.

We had a sinister ride by the uncertain light of a waxing moon. Very much afraid that Slimène might fall off his horse, anxious to know what the sheikh would do for us. We arrived at last, responded with impatience to the repeated greetings of Guezzoun and the other servants, and found ourselves seated all alone before the sheikh in that vast room with sand on the floor and low, powerful arches. A candle lit the great red carpet we were sitting on, which left the corners of the room in blurry shadows.

There was a ponderous silence. I could tell that my poor Rouh' could not speak and I myself felt as if I were being strangled.

I saw that Rouh' was crying and felt like bursting into tears myself.

Upset as I was, I tried for a long time to tell the sheikh about our predicament. He said nothing, looking overcome, as if his mind were elsewhere.

33

In the end the sheikh and I exchanged a glance. I tried to make mine as meaningful as possible in drawing his attention to Rouh', who was burning with fever and about to faint. The sheikh stood up and went into his house ... none too soon, for a glaze had come over Rouh's eyes by then.

A moment later the sheikh came back and put 170 francs in front of Rouh', saying: 'God will pay the rest.'

Without saying a word, without even taking the banknotes, Rouh' stared at them and began to laugh, a crazy laugh that frightened both the sheikh and myself.

I wondered whether he might be losing his mind altogether.

I stepped out for some air. From the rocky sand in front of me rose the eerie outlines of the little graveyard for the sheikh's children. Many an innocent creature lies asleep there; barely do these young souls come to life than they are whisked off again into the netherworld's dark, mysterious reaches. No sooner do their earthly eyes take in the sterile dunes along this vast horizon than they are dimmed at once.

I stopped among the piles of sand heaped up against the thick and heavily buttressed wall, and in that utter silence I saw a nocturnal animal I could not identify – perhaps a little desert fox – shoot by quite close to me. I raised my eyes to heaven and, on impulse, recited the fatiha under my breath.

I went back indoors. We left, feeling lighter of heart but wistful all the same ...

We were afraid we might lose our way among those vast stretches of cemetery and wan-looking dunes.

We did make our way home, though, via the village that lies to the east of the Ouled-Touati. As we came through the narrow path that overlooks the Hama Ayechi garden, the sight we saw was a curious one: the palm trees below us were all asleep in the shadows, yet there was the odd ray of silvery, occasionally vaguely pink light shining through their trunks.

It was nearly ten o'clock, and there was not a sound to break the silence in all that solitude and desolation.

The moon was setting as we entered the Ouled-Ahmed graveyard, and for an instant the only things visible by the great dune's ridge were the crescent's two red points, a strange and disquieting sight; then they were gone and there was nothing but night and darkness.

We hardly made any headway for fear of stumbling and falling, for that road is littered with graves. When we had set off after the maghreb, there had been lamps burning all through the cemetery in those tiny grey necropolises, wan little flames in the falling dusk: it was a Friday night.

Everything was in shadow again by now, the lights were out and all those graves were slumbering in darkness. Oh, the thought of leaving that place and perhaps never seeing it again!

These days so full of sorrow and uncertainty have made me realise just how much I love this part of the world; the loss of this land of sun, sand, lush gardens and winds will be a bitter one.

Studied those curious cemeteries, in particular the one south of Tarzout: its tombs like pointed belljars, tiny koubbas in the shape of fortified towers, and all that picturesque profusion of necropolises that surrounds the twin cities of Tarzout and Guémar.

Had no trouble finding Sidi-el-Hussein's dilapidated zawyia. Had a depressing conversation, in that shabby-looking room giving onto a vast courtyard littered with stones in all sorts of odd shapes.

By the time I went into the outer courtyard, I spotted Rouh's red silhouette taking off along the road toward the market, and sent Ali after him.

Hearing our tales of woe and looking at Rouh's deathly pale face, the good sheikh wept at the thought that we would soon be parted.

Many a memory has created a bond between him and us. The times I rode to Amiche and Ourmès with him, the long talks we had and the mystery of our joint efforts ...

We left shortly before 'asr. We said goodbye in the dunes near Kouinine. Together with Ali I took the westward road for El Oued, skirting Kouinine on my left. A handful of women in blue veils were on their way home, bending under the weight of their guerbas loaded to the brim.

No sooner had we passed Kouinine than I turned around

and took off at a gallop by myself, in hopes of catching up with Slimène.

It was too late and I came home by sundown via the deserted road along the Sidi Abdallah cemetery.

Isabelle describes the arrest of the man who made an attempt on her life, an event she will detail in full in Journal Three.

9 February 1901

Around five o'clock this afternoon, Abdallah Muhammad[28] was put in a prison cell.

I saw him arrive and studied him while he was being searched by soldiers ... I had a poignant feeling of profound pity for the man, for he is but the blind instrument of a destiny he does not understand. And at the sight of his grey silhouette standing there head bowed between those blue uniforms, I had a sense of *mystery* that may well have been the strangest and most profound I have ever experienced.

Try as I may to feel any, I cannot find hatred for this man in my heart.

What I do feel for him is curious: whenever I stop to think about it, I have the feeling that I am in the presence of a mystery which may well *hold the key to the entire meaning of my life.* As long as I do not fathom that enigma – and will I ever! God alone can tell – I shall not know *who* I am, nor the *reason* for my curious life.

If my strange way of life were merely a *pose*, one could indeed say: 'She has asked for it ...' But that is not the case! No one has ever lived as haphazardly as I do, and it is the inexorable chain of events that accounts for my being where I am, events that are not of my making.

Perhaps the strange side of my nature can be summed up in a single trait: the need to keep searching, come what may, for new events, and flee inertia and stagnation.

JOURNAL THREE

Isabelle starts her third journal in the French Military Hospital where she is recovering from the attempt on her life. She is physically weak and morally dejected. Slimène is in Batna, where she joins him when she is recovered. She does not keep a chronological journal but goes back and forth in time, describing the murder attempt later than her convalescence.

'In the name of God, the all powerful,
the merciful!'

El Oued (February 1901)

The long and sleepless winter night seems endless in this deadly silence. It is dark and stifling here in this tiny, narrow hospital ward. The night light on the wall near the window throws a feeble light on the seedy decor: humid walls with a yellow base, two white army beds, a small black table and boards to hold books and bottles. An army blanket hides the window. Not a sound in the barracks' vast courtyard.

From time to time my sensitive invalid's ear picks up long and far-off barking and all is silent once again. Then comes the sound of soldiers marching, a clicking of rifle butts, a brief, impersonal command, while more footsteps go off in the direction of the infantry barracks. There has been a changing of the guard at the gate.

I lie here and languish all by myself. My injured, shattered head is burning and as for my badly wounded arm, it is giving me a lot of discomfort, and feels terribly heavy. I keep moving it around with my good right arm as best I can, but I am in pain no matter what I do with it, a nauseating sort of pain.

37

The details of that fatal day all suddenly come back to me. There I was, having received a blow on the head. The murderer stood in front of me, his arms raised high up. I could not tell what it was he had in his hands. I then began to moan and I was overcome with pain and nausea. My thoughts became muddled and suddenly everything grew dim.

Through the window over the door I can see wan moonlight shine on the building opposite where the autopsy ward is located, with its metal table and boxes full of disinfectants. I may well soon be lying on that hideous table myself. Not that I am afraid of death. What I do dread is suffering, long and absurd stretches of it, and also something vague, dark and sinister that hovers near me, something invisible that only I can see . . .

And should it be written, should it be my destiny to die right here in this timeless desert, no brotherly hand would come to close my eyes . . . In that last moment on earth, no brotherly lips would utter words of love and consolation.

21 February 1901, noon

Yesterday I went to Guemar for a visit to Sheikh Sidi-el-Hussein.

The wind had thrown a shroud of grey dust over all the palm trees and once again played havoc with the dunes between Kouïnine and Tarzout. Those sad little towns, Gara, Teksebet, Kouïnine, all seem so much more desolate and deserted when the great winds of winter do their blowing.

The Souf now looks wan under the pallid sky, and the dunes are at their most lacklustre. In the evening I sometimes hear magic sounds coming from the Messaaba, the poignant music of a tiny Bedouin flute.

In a mere few days' time I shall no longer hear those distant sounds.

The sound of the toubib's humming this morning suddenly brought me back to my stay in Tunisia – however dead all that is now and deeply buried under so many layers of grey ash, just like my life in the Sahara soon will be too.

38

I remember that September night two years ago, when Ali and I were leaning on our elbows by the little window at La Goulette; on one side I could hear the soft murmur of the placid sea, and on the other the clear and innocent voice of Sidi Béyène's little Noucha singing that sad Andalusian song:

☾ *My mind is gone, my mind is gone!*

Ali's warm and passionate, sonorous voice then took over the wistful refrain, as if in a dream, and all I did was listen ...

There are moments when I am suddenly reminded of the recent past like that, a period I rarely think of nowadays. Memories of Tunis in particular come to haunt me. Meaningless, forgotten street names come to mind for no good reason.

I went to my house today, and had an awful feeling of emptiness.

Going through the door I felt an inward shudder and thought: 'Rouh will never come in here again ...'

Never will we lie in each other's arms again in that tiny white vaulted room of ours, and sleep in close embrace as if we somehow knew that dark and hostile forces were trying to come between us. Never again will sensual ecstasy unite the two of us under that roof we have both held so dear.

Yes, the end has come.

In four days' time I too will head north, a place I would have been too happy never to see again.

The last of my wistful childish whims is to ask for burial right here in these white sands gilded at dawn and dusk by the scarlet sun ...

This part of the journal was written down in Marseilles, six months after the events it describes.

Marseilles, 8 July 1901, 9 p.m.

Departure from El Oued on Monday 25 February 1901 at 1.30 p.m.

26th – Reached Bir-bou-Chama by maghreb.
Black sky, grey night, a strong and icy north wind.
Caravan: Bach-hamar Sasi. Deïras: Naser and Lakhdar.

39

Infantryman: Rezki, Embarek, Salem and El Hadj Mohammed, from Guémar. Two mental patients accompanied by a young man (from Algiers). Hennia, Spahi Zouazouë's mother and her son Abdallah.

27th – Left on the 27th around 7 a.m. Reached Sif-el-Ménédi by five in the afternoon. Road: trees, plains consisting of mica and of talc, scrubs; a handful of shotts in the vicinity of the borj.

Sif-el-Ménédi: a borj set on a very low cliff, scrubby horizon. Well-tended garden, salt-water ponds near by. Excellent impression, similar to that of the Oued Rir's salt oases. Lakhdar's dromedary took off in the evening, and the deïra went to look for it. I felt exhausted, headache (walked one third of the way). Sat on my bed and thought how nice it would be to live in that borj for a while, with the vast maquis for a horizon. Children singing in the garden.

Isabelle is making her way to Batna to join Slimène.

Chagga, Friday 3 March 1901, 9 p.m.

Spent the night at Stah-el-Hamraïa. Spent the evening in the borj's main hall, listening to Lakhdar and the camel-drivers sing.

Bedded down with Khelifa and infantryman Rezki.

Set out on horseback. Terrain that varied between the salty and rocky kind. Shrubs of broom with white flowers, Sahara trees, little shrubs with blue flowers. A few shotts, salty soil and yellow sand. Dismounted by the first guemira.

A little before the guemira, in the maquis on the left, is a wonderfully cool wellspring. Bought some hares from hunters. Set off again on foot. Encountered several caravans. Spotted the tent of a captain in the Engineer Corps at the bottom of a hillside on the left.

Once again we caught sight of shott Meriri, a sea without a horizon, a milky expanse dotted with white islets.

1 March, Chagga.

Bedded down in the little room to the left, Khelifa, Rezki and myself. In the large room next door are Hennia and her son. In the other one are the mental patients, their guide and the outcasts. The deïras sleep outdoors, with the camel-drivers, near the fountain.

In the nearby garden flooded with salt water, toads are croaking their melancholy song in the desert's silence.

All along the way this afternoon there was languorous bird song. Torrid heat all day.

Thought lovingly of the way the Sahara has bewitched me for life, and what bliss it will be to come back. Felt I was being bold in the face of destiny, and full of irrepressible energy.

Another thought has come to haunt me, and there is no sleep for my weary mind: there are ecstasies in store for me in Batna, and this is keeping me on tenterhooks of voluptuous expectation.

Day after tomorrow, that is to say in two days' time, I can give in to these physical cravings and spend whole nights in wild sensuality, the way we used to do in El Oued ... hold my master in my arms, hold him tight against the breast now suffering too much love and no gratification.

It has occurred to me tonight that I am still quite young, that life is not so black and dreary as all that and that I still have grounds for hope.

As long as the Sahara is there with its magnificent expanse, I will always have a refuge where my tormented soul can go for relief from the triviality of modern life.

Take Rouh' along to distant places, off into the desert, for the pursuit of bold adventures, and heady interludes.

Batna, 20 March, 11 p.m.

Reached Batna on the 18th at 8.30 p.m.

I do not mind the poverty, which has now become a fact, nor the cloistered existence among Arab women. I might even think it is a blessing to be so totally dependent on Rouh from now on. What torments me, though, and makes life almost unbearable is the sad and bitter fact that we are apart, and that I can only see him for a fleeting moment now and then. What do I care about the rest, when simply holding him in my arms as I did yesterday and looking into his eyes brings me back to life?

41

Without my being aware of it, the great love of my life, the one I did not think would ever appear, has actually come!

Batna, Tuesday 26 March, 1 p.m.

Took Souf for a ride today to the foot of the mountain, let the horse roam freely about the meadow, and stretched out underneath a pine tree.

I daydreamed with my gaze upon the great valley, the blue mountains opposite and Batna in its slum-like setting. A sensuous delight at being out of doors in the sun, far from the grey walls of my dreary prison. Everything is turning green again, the trees are in bloom, the sky is blue and countless birds are singing.

Where is that long-past autumn day when, eyes closed and with a peaceful heart (so much for human nature's utter blindness!) I listened to the strong wind rustle through the tough djerids of Debila's palm trees! Where is that Oued Souf of ours, with its white dunes and gardens, and Salah ben Taliba's peaceful house, a stone's throw from the dunes of Sidi-Mestour and the silent necropolis that is the Ouled-Ahmed's final resting place! Where is the land of holy zawyias and marabouts' graves, the harsh, magnificent land that feeds the flames of faith and where we found such bliss? Where is all that, and will I ever see it again?

Over here, my poverty is total ... No food, no money and no heat. Nothing!

The days all come and go, and blend into the past's black void; each new dawn brings us closer to the day of our deliverance, set for 20 February 1902, when real life will truly *begin* for the two of us at last.

Everything is in the hands of God, and nothing happens ☾ *against His will.*

Batna, Friday 12 April 1901, 5 p.m.

These days I go out every morning with my faithful Souf to spend a few hours of quiet in the open fields.

There I dismount and sit down by the edge of the road,

near a field of colza, at the foot of the dark Ouled-Abdi, for a smoke and time to dream; I hold on to Souf's bridle while he greedily grazes on the green blades of grass he carefully picks out among the flowers.

In the distance to the north, the outlines of the dreary city full of barracks and administrative buildings. My back is turned toward it and my gaze is on the countryside in bloom.

I have already come to know this place quite well, and it gives me moments of serenity and bliss.

The other night I was lying next to Slimène on Khelifa's mat. Through the window I could see the blue sky, a few clouds gilded by the setting sun, and the tops of trees that are suddenly green again: all of a sudden, I was reminded of the past, in a flash so keen it left me in tears. The overall landscape is so similar here that memories of *La Villa Neuve* keep haunting me.

Batna, 26 April 11 p.m.

I am feeling depressed tonight in a way I cannot define. I feel lonely without Ouïha, and cannot stand the boredom. Yesterday's storm has left Batna inundated, dark and freezing, and it is full of mud and filthy gutters. My poor Souf is very ill, so that I cannot even go for my strolls along the open road, or up to that desolate graveyard where damaged tombs, terrifying windows upon the spectacle of human dust, lie scattered among the fragrant tufts of grey chih near a green meadow full of purple flax, white anemones and scarlet poppies in full bloom.

The other day I wandered around among a crowd of Muslims brandishing the flags of ancient religious ceremonial occasions; to the accompaniment of tambours and flutes they prayed for rain, for an extension of their fleeting Algerian spring which already, in its haste to move on, is blending summer flowers with those of spring.

After six long days of only seeing Rouh' for brief and furtive moments by the gate of the hated barracks where he is quartered, he came to see me yesterday ... I held him in my arms and after the first wild, almost savage embrace, tears ran down our cheeks, and each of us felt a very

43

mysterious fear, even though neither of us had said a word or knew why.

I realised yesterday once again how honest and beautiful is my Slimène's soul, because of his joy that Augustin[30] was making up with me and was doing justice to us both. In spite of my past, present and future misfortunes I bless God and my destiny for having brought me to this desert and given me to this man, who is my *only solace*, my only reason for happiness in this whole world.

I have often been hard on him and unfair, I have been impatient for no good reason, so insane as to hit him, although secretly ashamed because he did not strike back but merely smiled at my blind rage. Afterwards I always feel truly miserable and disgusted with myself for the injustice I might have committed.

This afternoon I went to see the police official who is without a doubt an enemy spy in charge of keeping an eye on me. *He* was the first to come out with the theory that P[31] was the one who had wanted me killed, and that the murderer was bound to go scotfree. If so, that means I am doomed to die anywhere I go in the South, which is the only place where we can live.

If the crime committed at Behima is only slightly punished or not at all, that will amount to a clear signal to the Tidjanyas[32]: 'Go ahead and kill Si Mahmoud, you have nothing to fear.'

Yet God did stay the assassin's hand once, and Abdallah's sabre was deflected. If God wants me to die a martyr, God's will is bound to find me wherever I am. If not, the plots of all those who conspire against me will be their undoing.

I am not afraid of death, but would not want to die in some obscure or pointless way. Having seen death close up, and having felt the brush of its black and icy wings, I know that its proximity means instant renunciation of the things of this world. I also know that my nerves and willpower will hold out in times of great personal ordeals, and that I will never give my enemies the satisfaction of seeing me run in cowardice or fear.

Yet, as I think of the future, there is one thing that does frighten me: misfortunes that might befall Slimène or

Augustin. Faced with those, I would have no strength whatsoever. It would be hard to imagine worse poverty than the kind I am up against right now: yet the only reason it worries me is that our debts stand to spell disaster for Slimène.

Fortunately, my enemies think I am rich. I was right to spend money the way I did two years ago, here and in Biskra, for a reputation of wealth is just as useful for our defence as actual wealth would have been. Oh, if those rascals were to know that I am utterly destitute and that the slightest humiliation could be my undoing, they would not hesitate for a moment!

It is obvious that they are afraid. Otherwise they would arrest me as a spy, or expel me.

I was right to account for the wretched way I live down here as mere eccentricity: that way, it is not too obvious that I am in fact destitute.

I have begun to make a point of going to people's houses to *eat*, for the sole purpose of keeping fit, something that would have been *anathema* in the old days, like the other thing I have been doing lately, namely going to see marabouts, just to beg them for money.

I must have an iron constitution, for my health is holding up contrary to all expectation: those frightening last days in El Oued, the injury, the shock to the nervous system and the haemorrhage in Behima, the hospital, the journey, half of which I made on foot, my poverty here, the cold and the poor diet, which mostly consists of bread, none of that has got me down. How long will I be able to hold out?

How can one explain the fact that at home, where I had warm clothes, an outstandingly healthy diet, and Mummy's idolatrous care, the slightest chill I caught would degenerate into bronchitis; whereas here, having suffered freezing temperatures at El Oued, and at the hospital as well, having travelled in all kinds of weather, while literally always getting wet feet, going around in thin clothes and torn shoes, I don't even catch a cold?

The human body is nothing, the human soul is all.

Why do I adore Rouh's eyes so? Not for their shape or colour, but for the sweet and guileless radiance in their expression, which is what makes them beautiful.

45

The way I see it, there is no greater spiritual beauty than fanaticism, of a sort so sincere it can only end in martyrdom.

Isabelle was expelled from French North Africa after the trial of her would-be assassin.

Friday 3 May 1901, 9.45 a.m.

Found out last night that I am to be expelled again.

Everything has once again been shattered and destroyed.

I shall muster the courage needed to fight the injustice done to me, and hope to win with God's help.

Yet how can I go off, for God knows how long, and leave Rouh' with whom I am so close? How can I do without him?

Twice more shall we sleep in each other's arms. Twice more shall I see his beloved silhouette in the doorway of the shabby room we have come to cherish.

I will have the bliss of seeing Augustin again, but how can I survive without the presence of my sweet Zizou? His love and kindness have brought sunshine to this year's darkest hours; without him, all will be utterly gloomy.

After her expulsion, Isabelle makes her way once more to her brother's house in Marseilles.

6 May 1901

Left Batna and arrived at Bône at three in the afternoon. Spent the night of the 6th, the day and night of the 7th and 8th at Khoudja's house.

Written at Bône, 8 May 6 p.m.

No doubt about it, life without Slimène *will not do*. Everything is bleak and dreary, and time keeps dragging on. Poor Ouïha Kahla! Poor Zizou! When will I ever see him again?

Sailed from Bône on Thursday 9th May on the *Berry*, of the Compagnie Générale des Transports Maritimes. Travelled fourth class under the name of Pierre Mouchet, deckhand.[33] Reached Marseilles on Saturday 12th, at 3 p.m. Disembarked at Le Môle. Took the tramway to the Rue d'Oran.

Tomorrow, when I will have recovered a bit from all the fatigue of these last two days, I shall write down a detailed description of my impressions of Bône, the crossing and the first few days in Marseilles. Tonight I only want to go into the *psychological* aspect of my recent experiences, for having started out in tears and apprehension, things have now suddenly taken a pleasant, *useful* turn and brought me strokes of good luck as, for instance, my amazing encounter with my old friend Sousse Abd-el-Aziz-Agreby, an encounter that may well bring a considerable improvement in Ouiha's predicament and my own; perhaps he will wangle some concession from Algiers; perhaps he will find someone to take Slimène's place in Tunisia? He will quite probably start reimbursing me for part of what he owes me, little by little.

There has been no decree expelling me from the country. That means I can go back and join Slimène again as soon as I can find the means to travel, and the Military Court will provide me with those before June 18th. In the meantime I must sit down and do my Russian work and finish it, for which I have now got the time.

The horizon has cleared up a good deal all around. After my strange encounter with Abd-el-Aziz, I felt *true friendship* for him. A feeling of great happiness and real emotion.

Perhaps he was sent by God to help me through this difficult period in my life!

I think of Slimène, and this may well be the *first* time I do so in *reasonable* terms.

Yes, once I am back with him again, I must start behaving differently towards him right away, so that our happiness as a couple is not jeopardised, since marriage must not be based only on love. No matter how deep and strong, love alone is not a solid enough foundation. I must go out of my way to show him how devoted I am to him, and must let my kindness outweigh his bitter hardships.

I must learn to hold my temper and restrain my selfishness and violence in order not to tax his patience. I must learn the very thing that is hardest for someone of my temperament, namely obedience (which of course has its limits and must on no account turn into servility), thus making life so much easier for the two of us. To put it in a nutshell, I must change my ways and become easier to live with, which will not be too hard to do, what with Slimène's easy good nature and his patience.

Isabelle retrospectively describes her journey to Marseilles, starting from her departure from Batna.

I left the house on 6th of May at dawn; quiet in the streets. Went as far as the entrance to the railway station with Slimène, Labbadi and Khelifa. Sat briefly on a bench in Avenue de la Gare. I turned back one last time for another look at that beloved red silhouette as it already lost its contours in the shadows.

We parted without too much anguish, because we both had the feeling we would soon see each other again.

How I now miss Batna, city of sorrow, love and exile, where my poor good-hearted friend has stayed behind ... the same goes for Souf, my valiant and loyal horse, my mute companion on those unforgettable rides through the beloved dunes.

Bône's magic charm seems to have evaporated and I would not set foot in the place if it were not for ✝ *The White Spirit*'s grave!

Once on the *Berry* I sat up front, disguised as Pierre Mouchet in my wretched sailor's outfit, and felt as sad as an emigrant being banished from his native soil. I was suddenly unable to fight back my tears, and had no place to go and hide them. The other passengers all seemed surprised, but did not smile. Felt profound distress at the view of that lively, colourful quay, reddish ramparts, and sacred green hill with its black cypresses. Felt a sharp twinge of pain at the thought that there, in the early dusk, was Africa vanish-

48

ing from sight, the ardently beloved soil that harbours both the glorious Sahara and Slimène.

My stay in Bône was so brief and fleeting, and above all so agitated and tormented, it might as well have been a nightmare.

Sitting on my bundle by the windlass, I mulled over the hopeless poverty I have come to, the utter destitution that will now be mine. Thought also of the settings I grew up in, the days long past when I was well off and would indulge my taste for dressing as a sailor, of all things.

Made my bed on the spot because it offered a bit of warmth, and dozed off.

Was awakened by a violent storm. Took my rags under the bridge, near the lamp depot. Was told to scram, and wandered around in the torrential rain.

Found shelter near the bow at last, thanks to a kind-hearted sailor, together with two Neapolitans and an old man on his way back from Japan, dressed in a black Arab kachébia.

Set off in search of some water. Drank from the reservoir! Had a fairly good night, lying on the floor. Slept all of the next day (10 May) till four in the afternoon. We were about to hit bad weather; the elderly Neapolitan was feeling seasick. A heavy swell drove me behind the anchor windlass. The ill-tempered ship's boy put me on top of a pile of ropes, on the starboard side.

Violent storm all night long, much heavy tossing and pitching, huge amounts of water taken in by the bow and constantly crashing down on deck with a thunderous roar. An awful night; kept getting splashed, the wind kept wailing and howling, huge waves kept roaring and rumbling.

Of all the *desperately* lucid thoughts I had that night so full of fever and delirium, I remember one in particular:

'This is the voice of Death bellowing[34] and lashing out against the *Berry*, a poor little hull shaken and tossed about like a mere feather on these hostile waters.'

All the passengers from the upper deck went down to third class during the night. Was left all by myself, cut off by the constant cataracts thunderously heaving above my head and hitting the deck, which made it impossible for me to pass without running the risk of being crushed.

49

It was clear and sunny when we docked that afternoon. Quietly took the tramway and dragged my bags all the way on foot.

Stunned at the lack of news from Slimène. Awoke with a sudden start in the middle of the night, in such a state of anguish I almost went to wake Augustin.

Not a moment's peace all morning, till Slimène's telegram arrived. It gave me the courage needed to bear the latest of my ordeals, the hardest of them all: the fact that we are apart.

A sense of contentment over here, in finding, if not affluence, at least the security of a certain comfort that, compared to my own degree of poverty, feels like wealth.

Old lively memories have come back to me, of the time I spent here in November 1899. Listening to the Marseilles church bells just now took me back to those days when Popowa and I would wander around the city, a place I love dearly but would not want to live in.

Who will give me back my Souf, though, with its white zawyias, its tranquil homes and grey cupolas, its boundless sandy stretches? And who will give me back Slimène, the friend and lover who is all the family I have on earth?

(Copied and completed on 25th May.)

Marseilles, 3 June 1901, 9 p.m.

I want to leave as soon as I can, go and join Slimène and never leave him again; do all I can to keep him, for I now know that he is all I have left in this world and that life is not worth living without him. Augustin, to be sure, does all he can for me, but that marriage of his has put a permanent wedge between us, and I can no longer rely on him the way I used to feel I could. And then there is the *thoughtlessness* of that wife of his, which is to be expected from someone as vulgar as that, which rules out any life in common with them for me.

The only person with whom I have been able to live in harmony is Slimène. I look forward to the moment of our reunion as to a time of *deliverance*.

50

As it would in no way affect the impending trial, if the money from El Agreby comes in Wednesday's mail, I might leave for Philippeville on Saturday to be with Slimène a week earlier and cut short the state of anguish I have been in since leaving Batna a whole month ago.

I will have to try and organise my life there in such a way as to make it bearable, especially if we are to stay in Batna for a certain length of time. When I go back after the trial we will only have eight more months of misery ahead of us, at the end of which lies our marriage and freedom. God has always had mercy on us so far and has never let us down even when things were at their worst.

I find that I have been through a period of *incubation*, and the odd result is beginning to show: I have a better understanding of people and of things, and my life's outlook is less bleak, although still infinitely sad.

Life is not just a constant struggle against circumstances, but rather *against ourselves*. That's an age-old adage, but most people simply ignore it: hence all the discontent, evil and despair.

The mind has vast power over itself, and actually exercising that power enhances it further.

Suffering is often the very thing it takes to release that power. Suffering is a positive thing, for it sublimates the emotions and produces great courage or devotion; it creates the capacity for strong feelings and all-encompassing ideas.

I now see that there is one thing I have never understood and never will: *Augustin's character and the kind of life he leads*. Has he become like this, or has he always been this way? He is getting more and more set in his ways and stuck in his present situation, which leaves no room for any intellectual development and strikes me as being alien and unpalatable.

What, then, lies in store for his child who looks so like me and, I am sure, although I cannot say why, will have a character very similar to mine ... Poor little Helen, I feel both *touched* and *frightened* by the resemblance! No doubt you will never get to know me, for I shall not be a presence in the house where you will grow up.

What became of the *affinity* that existed between

51

Augustin's temperament and my own? The closer I look, alas, the less I can find it!

O Slimène, Slimène, stay the way you were for ten whole months; you are all I have left!

Marseilles, Tuesday 4 June, noon

Had a terrible night doubting everything, especially Rouh'; felt so tormented I thought I might lose my mind.

I blew out my lamp at two o'clock and dozed for a while. Woke up with a start at three o'clock feeling inexplicably frightened, a prelude to the hideous state of despair that lasted until broad daylight.

Irritability, anguish, frayed nerves and a grief so sharp I felt I might go mad; all the rewards of this latest visit here. And my heart yearns for Slimène more and more every day. There, too, I will know hardship, poverty, boredom and chronic deprivation ... But I will also have the vast solace of knowing he is there, seeing him and hearing him speak to me, of having someone in whom to confide all my troubles and thoughts, who understands me almost completely.

I have a glimmer of hope that there may be some Russian assignment for me, which would improve things considerably.

Oh! If Atabek were to send me 20 francs and Agreby 30, I could leave on Friday, go to Batna and put an end to this intolerable state of affairs.

Anything, my God, anything to see him again, even for the odd glimpse by the barracks gate, as when he was on duty during the week!

Marseilles, Friday 7 June 1901

May 6th, publication of my letter concerning the Behima episode in the *Dépêche Algérienne*.

Sent letter of rectification on the 7th.

TEXT OF BOTH LETTERS

Sir,

On June 18th next, a native by the name of Abdallah ben Si Mohammed ben Lakhdar, from the village of Behima

52

near El Oued (district of Tuggurt) will appear before the Military Court at Constantine for trial. He stands accused of murder, or rather of attempted murder, and his guilt is an established fact.

I myself was the victim of his deed, which almost cost me my life.

I have been quite surprised to find no mention of the affair in the Algerian press, despite the fact that it is one of the strangest and most mysterious cases ever to have been tried in an Algerian court. I can only suppose that the press has been left in the dark about the facts. I believe that for the sake of justice and truth the public ought to learn a number of details before it comes to trial. I would be most obliged if you would be so kind as to publish this letter under my name. The responsibility for its contents is entirely mine.

I should like to preface my story with a few facts, in order to clarify the tale that follows.

The investigating magistrates have repeatedly expressed their surprise at hearing me describe myself as a Muslim and an initiate of the Kadriya brotherhood at that; they also have not known what to make of my going about dressed as an Arab, sometimes as a man, and at other times as a woman, depending on the occasion, and on the requirements of my essentially nomadic life.

In order to avoid giving the impression that I am merely following in the footsteps of Dr Grenier[35] or that in donning a costume and adopting some religious label I might be inspired by some ulterior motive, I wish to state unequivocally that I have not been baptised and have never been a Christian; although a Russian citizen, I have been a Muslim for a very long time in fact. My mother, a Russian aristocrat, died in Bône in 1897 after having become a Muslim and now lies buried in the Arab cemetery there.

Consequently I have never had reason either to have to become a Muslim or to falsely pretend that I am one. My Algerian fellow Muslims are so well aware of this fact that Sheikh Muhammad-el-Houssein, brother of the naib of the Ouargla brotherhood, Si Muhammad Taïeb, has had no misgivings about initiating me himself once I had been given a preliminary initiation by one of his mokkadem.

53

The reason for my explaining all this is to nip in the bud any suggestion that the motive for Abdallah's attempt on my life lies in a fanatical hatred of anything Christian, for I am not a Christian and the Souafas, including Abdallah, all know it!

What follows is a description of the attempt made on my life, at three in the afternoon on 29th January. It took place in the house of a certain Si Ibrahim ben Larbi, a landlord in the village of Behima, 14 kilometres to the north of El Oued along the road to the Tunisian Djerid.

I had visited El Oued at the time of my first journey into the Constantine part of the Sahara, in the summer of 1899, and had a vivid memory of the area's immaculate white dunes, lush gardens and shady palm groves. In August 1900 I went to live there for an indefinite period of time. That was where I was initiated into the Kadrya brotherhood, and became a regular visitor to the three zawyias located near El Oued, having won the friendship of the three sheikhs, sons of Sidi Ibrahim and brothers of the late naïb of Ouargla. In January I accompanied one of them, Si Lachmi, to the village of Behima. He was on his way to Nefta in Tunisia with a group of khouans for a ziara at the grave of his father, Sidi Ibrahim. For reasons of my own I could not go as far as Nefta, but accompanied the sheikh to Behima where the pilgrims were to spend the night. I expected to return to El Oued that same evening with my manservant, a Sufi who had followed me on foot. We entered the house of the man named ben Larbi, and the marabout withdrew to another room for the afternoon prayer. I myself stayed in a large hall giving on to an antechamber that led into the public square, where there was a dense crowd and where my servant was looking after my horse. There were five or six Arab figures of note, both from the village and the surrounding area, most of them Bhamania khouans.

I was sitting between two of them, the owner of the house and a young tradesman from Guemar, Ahmed ben Belkassem. The latter had asked me to translate three commercial telegrams, one of which was badly written and gave me a great deal of trouble. My head was bent in concentration, and the hood of my burnous covered my turban, so that I could not see what was going on in front of me. I suddenly felt a violent blow to my head, followed by two more to my left arm. I looked up and saw a poorly-dressed man who was not a member of the group. He was waving a weapon above my head that I took to be a truncheon. I leapt to my feet and rushed to the opposite wall for Si Lachmi's sabre. The first blow had landed on the top of my head, however, and so had left me dazed. I sank onto a travelling trunk, with a sharp pain in my left arm.

A young Kadrya mokaddem named Si Mohammed ben Bou Bekr and a servant of Sidi Lachmi's named Saad disarmed the assassin, but he managed to free himself. When I saw him coming toward me, I stood up and tried to grab the sabre again, but could not because my head was spinning and the pain in my arm was too sharp. The man ran out into the crowd, shouting: 'I am going to get a gun and finish her off.' Saad then showed me a sword whose blade was dripping with blood, and said: 'That's what that dog used to attack you with!'

Alerted by the commotion, the marabout came running in, and he was immediately given the name of the assassin by the people who had recognised him. He sent for Behima's independent sheikh who, like the assassin, belongs to the Tidjanya brotherhood.[36] It is common knowledge that the latter are the Kadryas' staunchest adversaries in the desert. The sheikh in question stubbornly resisted the marabout's request with various ploys, telling him that the murderer was a sherif[37], etc. etc. The marabout publicly threatened to tax him with complicity in the eyes of the Arab Bureau, and insisted that the assassin be arrested on the spot and taken away. The sheikh finally did so, but with very bad grace.

The culprit was taken into the same room where I had been put down on a mattress. He first pretended to be mad, but was caught out by his own fellow citizens who knew him to be a sane and sensible figure. He then said God had sent him to kill me. I was fully conscious and knew that I had no idea who the man was. I began to interrogate him myself and he said he did not know me either, had never set eyes on me but had come to kill me nevertheless. He said that if he were set free, he would attempt it again. When I

55

asked him what he had against me, he replied: 'Nothing whatsoever, you have done me no wrong, I don't know you, but I must kill you.' When the marabout asked him whether he knew that I was a Muslim he said he did.

His father, when summoned, said they were Tidjanyas. The marabout forced the local sheikh to inform the Arab Bureau, and asked for an officer to come and fetch the culprit and start an investigation, and for a medical officer for me.

The investigating officer, a lieutenant from the Arab Bureau, and the doctor showed up by eleven o'clock. The doctor found my head wound and the injury to my left wrist to be superficial; I owed my life to sheer luck: a laundry-line just above my head had cushioned the first blow, which would otherwise have been certainly fatal. My left elbow, however, had been cut to the outside bone; both the muscle and the bone had been severely slashed. I had lost so much blood in the six hours that I was so weak I had to be kept in Behima for the night.

The next day I was taken by stretcher to the military hospital at El Oued, where I remained till February 26th. Despite Dr Taste's efforts, I left the hospital a cripple for life, unable to use my left arm for anything at all strenuous.[38]

At the time of my first journey I had run into difficulties with the Arab Bureau at Tuggurt, which oversees the one at El Oued, difficulties that were due solely to the suspicious attitude of the Tuggurt Bureau. The head of the Arab Bureau at El Oued, its officers, those at the garrison and the army doctor have all been extremely good to me and I should like to express my thanks to them publicly.

The investigation showed that for five days before committing his crime, Abdallah had tried to buy firearms, but had been unable to find any. The day we arrived in Behima, he had transferred his family – the poor devil has young children – and his belongings to the house of his father, where he had not lived for six years. Although both father and son were prominent Tidjanyas, they had both suddenly withdrawn from their brotherhood; the father told me he was a Kadrya, and the son told the investigating magistrate he was a member of the Mouley-Taïeb brotherhood. The police officer, Lieutenant Guillot, established that Abdallah was telling a lie.

A few days before I left El Oued there was a rumour among the native population that shortly before the crime Abdallah, who had been riddled with debts, had gone to Guemar (the Tidjanya centre) and that upon his return he had settled his debts and even bought a palm grove.

Abdallah's father went to Sidi Lachmi's zawyia, and said in the presence of witnesses that his son had been bribed to attack me, but that as he did not know the identity of the instigators, he was seeking permission to speak to his son in the presence of an official to urge him to tell all. The marabout advised him to go to the Arab Bureau. The old man also asked one of my servants if he could speak to me, and told me: 'This crime was not our doing'; he also said he was anxious to see his son and persuade him to come clean. Those are the facts.

Now it is clear that Abdallah was not motivated by any hatred of Christians, but that he was acting with premeditation and on behalf of other people. I told the investigating authorities that in my view the attempted murder can best be explained by the hatred the Tidjanyas feel for the Kadryas,[39] and that the reason for the Tidjanya kabal or khouans wanting to do away with me was that they knew their enemies loved me – witness the khouans' grief at hearing about the crime. As I passed through the villages around El Oued on a stretcher on my way to the hospital, the inhabitants, men and women alike, all came to the road to shout and wail the way they do for funerals.

I trust the Military Court at Constantine will not merely try Abdallah ben Mohammed and let it go at that, but will also attempt to clear up the mystery surrounding the affair.

It seems to me that Abdallah acted at someone else's behest, and I would not see much point in having him solely take the blame, nor would anyone else who cares about justice and truth.

It is not Abdallah who should be standing trial but rather those who were behind him, the true culprits, whoever they may be.

I trust, Sir, that you will not refuse to publish this letter in your worthy newspaper, for I believe it to be of some interest. From the political, if not the social point of view, the Algerian Tell is not all that different from the other

French provinces; however, the same cannot be said of the
Sahara, where life is very different indeed, to a degree that
people in France can hardly begin to imagine.

ISABELLE EBERHARDT

Marseilles, 7 June 1901

Sir,

I should like to thank you most sincerely for having
published my long letter dated May 29th. I should add that
I could hardly have expected less from a newspaper with
your reputation for impartiality: the Dépêche Algérienne
has always shown considerable moderation, compared
with the excesses that have unfortunately become standard
policy for other Algerian publications. It seems to me,
however, that as the question of foreigners residing in
Algeria is such a burning topic at the moment, I ought to
expand upon my earlier letter for those who have taken the
trouble to read it.

You have credited me with an honour I do not deserve in
the least – that is, your assertion that I have a certain
degree of religious influence on the native population in the
district of Tuggurt. In actual fact I have never had, nor
tried to have, any political or religious role, for I feel I have
neither the right nor the requisite competence to meddle
with anything as serious and complex as matters of religion
in areas of that nature.

At the time I set off for Tuggurt in 1899, I felt it was my
duty to go and see Lieutenant-Colonel Tridel, who was in
charge of the district of Biskra, and inform him of my
departure. This officer gave me a most cordial reception
and, with military forthrightness, asked me point-blank
whether I was an English Methodist by any chance. I
showed him my papers, which are all in order and which
leave no doubt about the fact that I am Russian and have
permission from the imperial authorities to live abroad. I
also gave Lt. Col. Tridel my opinions on the subject of
English missions in Algeria, and told him that I have no use
for proselytising of any sort and certainly not for that brand
of hypocrisy that is so characteristic of the English and holds
even less appeal for Russians than it does for the French.

58

The officer I found to be in charge of the Arab Bureau in Tuggurt in the absence of the commanding officer was a captain by the name of De Susbielle, a strange and, if I may say so, awkward figure. Once again I had to establish that I was no English miss in Arab disguise, but a Russian writer. One would think that if there is one country where a Russian ought to be able to live without being suspected of dubious intentions, that country should be France!

The officer in charge of the El Oued Bureau, Captain Couvet, saw for himself over a six-month period that there was nothing to be held against me, apart from my eccentricity and a lifestyle that is perhaps a bit unexpected for a young girl like myself, but quite innocuous just the same. It did not occur to him that my preferring a burnous to a skirt, and dunes to the homestead could present any danger to the public welfare in the district annex.

As I have stated in my earlier letter, both the Souafas belonging to Sidi Abd-el-Kader's brotherhood and those of other ones friendly to it have all let me know how sorry they were to hear there had been an attempt on my life. The reason these good people all had a certain affection for me is that I had helped them as best I could and had used what little medical knowledge I had to treat the ophthalmia, conjunctivitis and other complaints that are endemic to the area. I had attempted to be of some help in my vicinity, and that was the extent of my role in El Oued.

Hardly anyone in the world is without a passion or mania of some sort. To take as an example my own gender, there are women who will do anything for beautiful clothes, while there are others who grow old and grey poring over books to earn degrees and status. As for myself, all I want is a good horse as a mute and loyal companion, a handful of servants hardly more complex than my mount,[40] and a life as far away as possible from the hustle and bustle I happen to find so sterile in the civilised world where I feel so deeply out of place.

I am not involved in politics, nor am I an agent for any particular party, for as I see it, they are all mistaken in their exertions. I am just a dreamy eccentric anxious to lead a free, nomadic life, which I hope to try and describe in writing some day. The intrigues, stratagems and betrayals

59

*that characterise Le Roux's Sonia are as alien to me as is
her character as a whole. Nor do I bear the faintest resemblance to the English Methodist I was taken for.*

*It is of course true that in the summer of 1899 it was
unusually hot in the Sahara, and that mirages will distort
many a perspective and account for many an error!*

I.E.

At long last I am almost certain of being able to leave on
Friday. That means being here for only another seven days.
I am sure that Augustin will do all he can to procure me the
money I need.

Poor Augustin! However enigmatic he may seem, he is
good to me and nothing in the world will ever succeed in
killing the deep and everlasting affection I feel for him. Oh!
what a pity that marriage of his makes it impossible for
him to come and join Slimène and myself for a truly wonderful life!

It is best, though, for everyone concerned that I leave,
and at the end of this week I shall have the inexpressible
joy of seeing Slimène again, of holding him in my arms and
☾ if Allah is willing, never leaving him again.

Spent the better part of last night feeling abominably ill;
dizziness and awful headache.

Once in Batna, I will have to do my best to save every
penny I can, be reimbursed as much money as possible and
above all, work in Russian: that way lies the only chance I
have of earning an income fairly soon. That will not be too
trying, providing my health holds out after the frightful
shocks it has had. To work so that I can stay with Ouïha,
that is my duty. He will some day find a way to make it up
to me for the hard work I shall do.

This evening I wrote a letter for Ahmed Cherif and as I
was doing so, I remembered the Autumn of 1899.

What became of the life of mystery and adventure I led
then in the Sahel's vast olive groves?[41]

How very strange the names I knew so well now sound
to me: Monastir, Sousse, Moknine, Esshyada, Ksasr, Ibellal,
Sidi N'eidja, Beni-Hassane, Anura, Chrahel, Melloul, Grat-
Zuizoura, Hadjedj ... What became of that incomparable
country, an African version of Palestine with its lush green

meadows and little white villages lying reflected in the blue water of its tranquil bays?

What became of Sousse, with its Moorish white ramparts and revolving beacon, and of Monastir, where waves never cease to roar and break upon the reefs?

Isabelle returns to Constantine to attend her aggressor's trial. She describes her arrival in Constantine, her meeting with Slimène, the arrival of Si Lachmi and his Khouans, and the trial.

Arrived in Constantine on Saturday 15th at ten past nine. Went to the Café Zouaouï. Set out with Hamou the porter to look for Ben-Chakar. Located him around noon. In the evening, Café Sidi Ksouma. Sunday 16th, six o'clock train, met Ouiha. Night at Hôtel Metropole, rue Basse Damremont. Monday 17th, arrival of Sidi Lachmi.

The 18th, 6 a.m. – Trial. Came out at eleven. Thursday 20th, left for Philippeville at 6.30. Arrived there at 9.35. Night at Hôtel Louvre.[42]

Before leaving, she made the following statement concerning her expulsion:

ISABELLE'S STATEMENT

As I have already pointed out, both to the investigating authorities and in my two letters to the Dépêche Algérienne, I have always thought, and will continue to think that Abdallah ben Si Mohammed ben Lakhdar was a mere tool in the hands of others who felt it was in their interest, real or imaginary, to get rid of me. It is obvious that if he was indeed bribed to kill me, which is what he told his father at the time of his arrest, he could not expect to reap any benefits from his deed, for he committed it in a house full of people whom he knew to be on friendly terms with me. He knew he would be arrested, in other words. It is therefore clear that Abdallah is mentally unbalanced and a lunatic. He has said he is sorry and even asked me for forgiveness during the trial. I therefore feel that today's

61

verdict is out of all proportion, and wish to state that I deplore its severity. Abdallah has a wife and children. I am a woman and can only feel bottomless pity for the widow and orphans. As for Abdallah himself, I feel deeply sorry for him.

At the end of this morning's trial I have had the painful surprise of learning that the Governor-General has issued a decree expelling me from the country. According to the terms of the decree, I am being banned from all Algerian territory, whether under civilian or military control. I can only wonder about the rationale for this measure. I am a Russian citizen and can in all good conscience say that I have done nothing to deserve it. I have never participated in or had any knowledge of any anti-French activities either in the Sahara or in the Tell. On the contrary, I have gone out of my way to defend the late naïb of Ouargla, Sidi Mohammed Taïeb, who died a hero's death fighting alongside the French, against the accusations made by a handful of Muslims who have argued that the naïb had betrayed Islam by installing the French at In-Salah. Wherever I have been, I have always spoken favourably of France to the natives, for I consider it my adoptive country. That being so, why am I being expelled? Not only does this measure offend my Russian sensibilities, it also puts me in a particularly painful situation as it will separate me from my fiancé for months to come; he is a non-commissioned officer at the Batna garrison, and is therefore not free to leave. I could perhaps have understood my being banned from territories under military control, in order to avoid my falling victim to revenge from Abdallah's tribe. I have no intention of returning to the South, however. All I ask is to be allowed to live in Batna and marry the man who was at my side during my ordeal and is my only source of moral support. That is all . . .

Thursday 4 July 1901, noon

Zouïzou has left on the *Touareg*. Day of gloom, utter boredom, anguish and despair. When will we see each other again?

Isabelle now returns to a description of her previous arrival in Algeria.

I had that feeling of well-being, of *rejuvenation* I always get when reaching the blessed coast of my African fatherland, a feeling so at odds with the way I react every time I reach Marseilles. My arrivals here are as depressing as the ones over there are cheerful!

Mountains, fertile slopes and plains until Constantine's magnificent rocks appeared on the horizon at last.

We disembarked at the station. I went into the Café Zouanouï at last, feeling embarrassed with my roumi's cap on. Stayed for quite a while and talked with the owner, an inveterate smoker of kif. I then set out with hamel Hantou to look for Mohammed ben Chakar. Steep and narrow winding streets, squares on a slope, intricate cross-roads, silent, shady corners, the immaculate, ornately carved porchways of old mosques, covered bazaars, it all went to my head the way ancient Arab decors always do.

We wandered around and asked ... At long last we found Ben Chakar's abode: way at the top of an alleyway's steps, a cul-de-sac with a floor made of wooden beams above it at barely six feet above the ground, the floor of a dark sort of den where one had to walk bent over for four or five yards. Suddenly we came upon a Moorish interior, bluish-white in colour just like the ones at Bône.

Mohammed ben Chakar's brother smokes chira as well as kif; he sometimes works as a porter, sometimes as a café-owner or a fritter-vendor, very congenial. Nice too was his wife, bright and mannish.

In the afternoon Ben Chakar and I set off for the Gorges du Rhummel, vertiginous chasms with frail-looking bridges hung across them, often in the shadows, subterranean stairways and endless labyrinths.

Met a few Constantinian craftsmen. Went to the Jewish baths, had great fun splashing about like overgrown children. Came back by the road above the abyss, along the shore opposite the city.

Went to Sidi Ksouma's café in the evening, and had the

distinct feeling that *Zouïzou was in Constantine*. Sat in a corner in my Arab garb, which made me feel at ease, and listened to the singing and beating of the tambourine until quite late. Feast of Beldia, pale, distinguished faces, empty of expression, eyes half-closed ...

Had a bad night, due to anxiety and *fleas* ...

Sunday, 16 June – Went to the station in vain.

By evening, still no news from Zouïzou; in desperation went to the station with Elhadj at 6.35 p.m. to meet the train from Philippeville. In discouragement we sat down on a stone and waited. Elhadj spotted Ouïha at last, in native civilian garb. Went for supper at Ben Chakar's, dressed as a Moorish woman and after that went to the Hotel Metropole, far away in the Rue Basse-Damrémont.

A night of bliss, tenderness and peace.

Early next morning, Monday 17th, went to the station to meet Sidi Lachmi. Spotted the tall figures of the Souafa witnesses in front of the station: Hama Nine, Muhamad ben Bou Bekr and Ibrahim ben Larbi.

Felt terribly moved at the sight of those *countrymen* of mine, who spoke with their local accent and all embraced me with tears in their eyes.

Went out onto the platform with the group of Souafas to welcome our beloved Grand Sheikh,[43] who smiled when he saw me.

Went on an endless search for a hotel with Hama Nine. Hostile refusals everywhere. Found temporary accommodations at the Metropole at last. Felt very comforted in being reunited with the sheikh, Bechir and all the others. Problems at the hotel. Transfer of the Nomads' *Zawyia* to the Hotel Ben Chimou, on the Marché du Chameau, near the theatre.

Spent the night in some Jewish furnished room, 6 Rue Sidi-Lakhdar, on the second floor.

On Tuesday the 18th, we arrived at the courthouse at 6.30 a.m. The guard brought me a cup of coffee in the witnesses' waiting room where I was by myself, an object of curiosity for the growing crowd of passers-by, officers, and ladies.

I saw Abdallah, in handcuffs, flanked by an escort of Zouaves.

Captain Martin, the Government Commissioner, came to shake my hand, as did his sister. At seven o'clock, the bailiff came to fetch me. The courtroom was packed. I did not feel too intimidated, and sat down next to Sidi Lachmi. Our two chairs faced the double row of witnesses on their benches. Not exactly run of the mill, those witnesses in their box: tanned, expressive faces, garbed in clothes either white or dark, with a single contrasting burnous the colour of blood, one worn by that traitor Mohammed ben Abdel-rahman, sheikh of Behima. Sidi Lachmi was dressed in green and white.

The court: a group of uniforms, medal-bedecked torsos, stiff and impassive in their attitude. Arms were presented; the presiding judge timidly opened the trial with a frail and quavering voice. The court clerk read the charges and called out the witnesses' names, starting with myself. We then were made to file out of the room one by one.

In the witnesses' room, Captain Gabrielli and the young lieutenant who is his secretary came to shake my hand. We talked for quite a while. Someone came to fetch me.

The judge was about to call the witnesses. The bailiff told me to stand in front of the presiding judge, and I was made to repeat the oath.

Still shy, the judge kept stammering as he questioned me on the basis of his notes. It did not take long. The interpreter called Abdallah and asked him: 'Have you anything to say to so-and-so?' 'No', was Abdallah's firm and simple reply despite everything that had been said, 'all I have to say is that I ask her to forgive me.'

I returned to my seat. Sidi Lachmi came in and testified in a simple and unruffled way. After that came the sheikh, who was followed by Ben Bou Bekr, Ibrahim ben Larbi, and then the assassin's father, simpering as usual.

After a five-minute recess we heard Captain Martin's speech for the prosecution which, although based on a theory that must be erroneous, was a vibrant plea in favour of the Kadryas and myself. The lawyer for the defence, whom I could not bear, spoke next. Reply from Captain Martin, and further words from the lawyer. The court withdrew. The room was buzzing with voices.

Isabelle begins to experience feelings of mysticism during this period.

8 July, 2 p.m.

I am going through a period of composure, both physical and emotional, of intellectual awakening and hope *without frenzy*, and time is going by fairly fast, which is the main thing just now.

Since that notorious trial in Constantine, I have felt a strong literary urge coming to the fore. My gift for writing is really reviving these days. I used to have to wait, sometimes for months on end, to be in the mood to write. Now I can almost sit down and write any time I want. I think, in fact, that I have reached a point where the potential I had been aware of all along has now begun to blossom.

As for my religious feelings, my faith is now truly genuine, and I no longer need to make the slightest effort. Before I go to sleep at night, I look deep down into my conscience, and never fail to find the blissful peace there that comes from the mysterious knowledge that will henceforth be my strength.

Two things are holding my attention at the moment: first my need for progress in the intellectual domain.

I must read certain books, in the vein of *Essais de psychologie contemporaine* by Bourget. As soon as I am settled in, I must register with a good library and re-read the *Journal des Goncourts*, which had such a good effect on me last year, as well as other works likely to improve my intellect.

The other question on my mind is of a very different order, one I would not dare come out with, except when talking to Slimène, for he will be the *only one to understand* and go along with it; and that is the question of becoming a *maraboute*,[44] a thought that came to me out of the blue the day Abdallah was taken from the civilian prison and put into his cell ... And Slimène had suspected it, by intuition, no doubt because we are so very close!

It seems to me that if I apply a great deal of willpower, I will have no trouble reaching a spiritual goal like that; it would give me infinite satisfaction and would open up unforeseen possibilities. ☽ *Lead us along the straight path*, and I believe that for me the straight path lies in that direction.

God planted a fertile seed in my soul: utter indifference to the things of this world, faith, and a boundless love and pity for suffering of any sort. The way I forgive evil is an expression of my unlimited devotion to the cause of Islam, which is the most magnificent of all because it is that of Truth.

Oh, the long hours I spent in those woods so full of mystery and shadows, the sleepless nights gazing at a cosmos full of stars. I must have been headed for religious mysticism already at the time!

A different choice in life companion would certainly have thwarted the necessary progress toward a future of that sort. Slimène will follow me wherever I go, and of all the men I have known, he is the *only true* Muslim, for he *loves* Islam with all his heart and is not content with paying it mere lip service.

A scientist, psychologist or writer reading these lines would be sure to say: 'She is out of her mind!' Yet the fact remains that if ever there was a time when my intelligence was burning like a flame, that time is now, and what is more, I know that I am only on the threshold of a new life.

Maître de Laffont unwittingly hit upon a truth when he said that I ought to be grateful to Abdallah. That I am, yes, and what is more, I *sincerely love Abdallah*, for he *was* the heavenly emissary he said he was.

It is likely that others were behind his deed, people who are the true culprits; he himself, however, must have been sent by God, for ever since that fateful day in Behima I have felt my soul move into a whole new phase in its earthly existence. In some mysterious way, Abdallah's life-long suffering will no doubt pay for the redemption of another's life.

What he has wrought will one day emerge from the shadows where I keep it hidden. That is my secret, one I must not reveal or talk about, except with the one man who discovered it all by himself one day.

All those who in their blindness think they have eyes to see may shrug or smile in the presence of the couple that we

67

form. It is a union based on sentiments and aims that have nothing in common with those marriages of theirs, motivated as they are by base ambition or infantile lust. Ours is a love *beyond* their understanding.

Thursday 11 July 1901, 9 p.m.

I am not in the mood right now to go on with my description of the trial. For the moment other thoughts and other memories have come to haunt me.

Felt bored and ill at ease last night, just like the day before. Anxiety this morning and much physical tension in the absence of any letter from Ouïha.

Went down to the Cours du Chapitre around 9.30 this morning to post a letter to Zouïzou. In the afternoon I started on my Russian assignment without much conviction. Had a good letter at last by three o'clock. The question of Zouïzou's replacement has *definitely* been settled and his return is now only a matter of days; time will pass by very quickly, now that I *know* he is coming.

What a sigh of relief we will heave, my God, after our visit to city hall, which will bind us to each other at long last and mean that others are *obliged* to treat us as a couple. God treated us that way and gave us his blessing a long time ago, in the form of love. Now men will soon lose the right to part us!

Memories are haunting me ... Geneva, times of anguish and of joy in my Russian way of life out there; the moment of my sailing for the beloved, fateful land of Barbary whence I have now been banned, but where I shall soon be able to return with my head held high ☺ if it pleases Allah!, and white Algiers, where I used to lead a double life, an unorthodox and heady one among people who had respect and even admiration for me, even though they knew nothing about me, not even what my gender was! Strange, intoxicating rides with Mokhtar, kif-smoking sessions ... the way we sang sad Algerian songs on our strolls along the quays ... the white Zawyia of Sidi Abd el-Rahman ben Koubrine, miniature city of one's dreams basking in the sunset above the fragrant Jardin Marengo ... the ecstasy felt during the icha prayer hour in the Jadid

Mosque ... Tuggurt asleep in its desert of salt, with its mirror image in the sluggish waters of its shott ... and farther on, the goal of that long journey, the splendid outline of the one and only City, the city of my choice, predestined El Oued!

Monday 15 July 1901, 11 a.m.

Felt very odd last night, for no discernible reason: a memory of my arrival at Sousse, two years ago ... and the desire to travel by myself to some uncharted place in Africa, where no one knows me, the way no one did when I came to Algiers last year ... but with adequate means this time.

Generally speaking, I feel a desire for mental *isolation*, although not for long, for I still miss Slimène. I would like to have a month all to myself before his return, and the necessary funds for a leisurely voyage by myself ... I know I would come back with very valuable, pertinent observations.

Yet this is a period in which my outlook is lucid and level-headed, and above all it is a period of work. The hope that a better life is just around the corner has of course a good deal to do with my present frame of mind.

It will soon be six months since that fateful episode at Behima. Even though I did not realise it then, that day was the beginning of another period of incubation, of the sort I have experienced all my life, for quite clearly my intellectual development has always been achieved by *fits and starts*: periods of restlessness, discontent and uncertainty have always been followed by the emergence of a better version of myself. A subject to be analysed, and described perhaps in a short story or a novel.

During the six or seven months we will have to spend here we must come to a definite decision about our future, and I must also devote that time to literary work of every sort.

Since I left for Bône in 1897 – how long ago that seems, alas! – I have neglected an art I love, namely drawing and painting. I plan to take them up again and while here will try to take a few lessons and acquire some instruction in portraiture and genre painting.

Our life, our *real* life will not take off again till after 20th February 1902.

If the Moscow business is settled by then in the form of a pension,[45] the best thing would be to go and create a peaceful haven for ourselves somewhere in the Tunisian Sahel – if it is not, the only feasible thing would be a career as an interpreter for a few years, somewhere in the South, it does not matter where exactly – a few years of living in the Desert, which would be wonderful too.

The time has now come to face the fundamental question of what my life is all about ... All the things that have happened so far have been mere passing phases ... ☽
And Allah knows all that is hidden in the heavens and on earth.

Tuesday 23 July

Over here,[46] we have now reached the depths of poverty, which is all the more frightening as there is nothing I can do; had I been surrounded by people like myself, I could perhaps have managed on tiny sums to provide for tiny needs. But such is not the case, and they have got appearances to keep up. For Slimène and myself, though, the end of our woes is near. I still need to lend a helping hand here, though, and that will not be easy. With what Slimène will earn and my way of keeping house, the two of us can scrape by in peace without giving up what little we need ... How will it all work out, though?

There will be no way out if they do not accept to have their meals with us, for I will never have enough money to support two households. As soon as Zouïzou gets here, he and I will have to discuss it, unless the steps I must try and take *vis-à-vis* Reppmann turn out to be successful. In that case I will then let them have all of what Reppmann sends me, and they will then have at least the wherewithal to manage for a month, a month and a half, if Reppmann agrees to lend me 100 rubles, which is nearly 250 francs. That would save us all, for it would give the two of us a chance to set up our own little household, and buy the few things I need. Once I dress as a woman, I am bound to find a little odd job while waiting for something better.

With that in mind, I must make good use of the last few days of solitude I have left and progress with my literary work as much as I can, write a few articles and copy them out, so that if I get any favourable replies from any quarter, I will have something to show and will not have to do any writing at the outset of our life together; that way I will not miss any opportunities that might turn up with newspapers and magazines after the summer.

There was a violent wind as I went to post a letter to Slimène, which may or may not reach him. I have very little hope. I went to Arenc on foot, and walked home via the Bar d'Afrique.

I will see tomorrow whether I can't earn a few pennies here and there writing letters in Arabic. I rather think that I am not going to lose heart. The one I fear for is Augustin. I just pray he will not think of doing what Volodia[47] did when he was down and out! As long as I am in the house, a collective suicide is out of the question. But after that?

☽ *May it please Allah* that we have seen the last of sombre dramas.

A thought to consider, which I found in *Notebook* I:
Do as much good as you can today,
For tomorrow you may die.
(Inscription on the Calvaire de Tregastel, Trécor, Britanny) which is a paraphrase of the words of Epictetus:
Behave as if you were to die the very next moment.
Few people could survive my lot.

I have now reached the depths of poverty, and may well be going hungry soon. Yet I can honestly say that I have never, not even for a moment, entertained the notion of doing what so many hundreds of thousands of women do. That is *out of the question*, period.

To say ☽ *There is no God but God and Muhammad is his prophet* is not enough, nor even to be convinced of it. It takes more than that to be a Muslim. Whoever considers himself to be a Muslim must devote himself body and soul, to the point of martyrdom if need be, to Islam for all time; Islam must inhabit his soul, and govern every one of his acts and words. Otherwise, there is no point in mystical exercises of any sort.

God is Beauty. The word itself contains everything:

Virtue, Truth, Honesty, Mercy. Inspired by such faith, a man is strong ... His strength may even seem to be supernatural. He becomes what they call a Marabout. As the knowledgeable and inspired Sheikh Ecchafi'r put it: 'Whatever you do, wherever you go, say: "Bismillah al-Rahman al-Rahim".' What he meant though, was not merely to *say*: in the name of Allah, when one undertakes something, but to actually do things *only* in the name of God, to do only what is true and good.

Those are things I thought about for years, and after Behima, I have come to understand them; no doubt the uninitiated, in their mindless craving for hollow phrases with which to mouth empty formulas, will shrug them off as mystical. If, as I hope and *think I can forsee*, it is written that I will complete the blessed cycle, it will be through Suffering, a path to which I sing a hymn of gratitude beforehand. One thing is certain, though, and that is that my soul has at last emerged from the gloom where it dwelt for so long.

Thursday 25 July, around 11 p.m.

Isabelle's depression increases as her relations with her brother and sister-in-law deteriorate.

I am finding it more and more difficult to stay here, especially in the absence of Rouh . Neither Augustin nor Hélène[48] is capable of loving me, nor will they ever be, for *they will never understand me.* Augustin has become deaf and blind to all of the sublime things I have understood at last.

I feel *alone* here, more so than anywhere else. The end of the month is in sight, though, and it cannot be long now before Zouïzou comes to put an end to my torments.

Received the two issues of *Les Nouvelles* from Algiers, dated July 19th and 20th, which carry the text of *El-Magh'reb* and *Printemps au Désert.*[49] I feel comforted by that success, and it does open up some possibilities at least. It means that I must have patience all the way and persevere. Above all, however, I must make up my mind to be aloof and stop discussing my affairs and ideas with people who do not *understand* them and do not *want* to.

No doubt about it (appearances these last two years notwithstanding), it seems destined that of all the people who lived the abnormal existence at the *Villa Neuve*, I am the *only one* whose soul might be saved.

I am not asking God for very much: simply that Slimène comes back, that we be married, that there be an end to this state of affairs over here: let Augustin and his wife find a way out! May they have enough to live on, especially as I have no way of helping people so diametrically opposed to me in every conceivable way.

Friday 26th, 10 p.m.

To close this chronicle of the last six months of my life, which I began in sadness and uncertainty in hospital, I have nothing but dreary things to report, although my spiritual progress remains steadfast. Of course the reason for my depression of the last three or four days lies in my environment and its insoluble financial problems. At bottom my soul is serene.

The only thing I find really hard to bear is the delay in Slimène's return, and the enormous effort it costs me to be patient. Now more than ever I am in need of his beloved presence. My heart overflows with love and I feel irresistibly drawn toward him, for he is the last refuge I have left on earth.

Having switched places with someone else, Slimène was drafted into a regiment of Dragoons stationed in Marseilles, where he and Isabelle were officially married.

Saturday 29 October 1901, 4 p.m.

The terrors of three months ago are now mostly gone from our horizon.

On the 17th of this month we officially became man and wife, never to be parted again. I am no longer forbidden to enter Algeria and in any event my period of exile is almost over: we will be off to our beloved land across the sea a month from now.

The following entry was added by Isabelle seven months before her death.

I have not recorded the thoughts I had in January 1902 ...
What does it matter? Three years later, in a different place
of exile, in the midst of poverty just as wretched, of solitude just as hopeless, I see what ravages time has wrought
in me ...

Many other corners of the African continent still hold
me in their spell. Soon, the solitary, woeful figure that I am
will vanish from this earth, where I have always been a
spectator, an *outsider* among men.

JOURNAL FOUR

Isabelle retraces the period she spent in Marseilles after being forced out of North Africa, while she awaited Slimène's transfer and their marriage.

'In the name of God, the all powerful, the merciful'
THOUGHTS AND IMPRESSIONS

Begun in Marseilles, 27 July 1901. Finished at Bou Saada on 31 January 1903.

In memory of ✝ the White Spirit

Marseilles, 27 July 1901

After several days of anguish, I got up this morning feeling full of energy again, of patience, and of an eagerness to get down to work.

If the torture of waiting for Slimène could only come to an end, if I knew the *exact date* of his arrival, this could prove to be one of the best periods of my life from the spiritual point of view.

In the autumn there will probably be some funds, which means the end of many a problem, and above all the end of my feeling so powerless. Oh! to come into the money for that hapless *Villa Neuve* at long last and go to see Africa once again, who knows, perhaps even the unforgettable Souf at that! To be able to read again, write, draw and paint, enjoy the intellectual side of life and lay the groundwork for my literary career. Should I be reasonable and, instead of going to Algeria, go to Paris with a certain number of articles for sale?

Slimène, who suffered from tuberculosis, was hospitalised during this time.

1 August 1901, 11 a.m.

Had a letter from Slimène yesterday that has upset everything one more time. He has been in hospital since the 28th. How could I ignore those mysterious premonitions I have had all these years about the stages of my *via dolorosa*!

I am shaking from head to foot. Yet I must sit down and write, copy the text of *Amiria* and send it off to Brieux.

The same day, half-past midnight[50]

Slimène, Slimène! I do not think I have ever loved him as deeply and as *chastely* as I do now, and if God wants to take him from me, let His will be done. After that I will undertake to go where there is fighting in the south-west, and die there no matter what, proclaiming ☾ *that there is no God but Allah and Muhammad is his Prophet.* That is the only death worthy of me and of the man I love. Any attempt to make a new life for myself would be in vain, and criminal as well.

Slimène wishes he had known my mother, but perhaps he will soon be with her. He can then tell her our two hearts are *united for all time*, and how much they have suffered here below.

You who are up there, White Spirit, and you, Vava, no doubt you can both see the tears I am shedding in the silence of the night, and you can read deep down into my heart. You know that at his side I have purified my poor soul in suffering and persecution, that I have not surrendered and that my heart is pure! See for yourself, and as you have left us to fend for ourselves in this world so full of woe, call for God's mercy now on the two of us, mercy from that same God who put the White Spirit to rest among the faithful. Call for His punishment, too, on those who hound us with such venom.

Why did I not do as I had wanted and go off with Sidi Muhammad Tayeb, why did I not go and die with him at Timmimoun? Why did fate have to take that poor child

76

away from the peaceful existence that was his, to make him share the doom that will be mine and saddle him with so much suffering and, perhaps, an early death?[51] Why should I not go off by myself? Does he regret having loved me, regret having suffered this much on my account?

Who will ever guess how infinitely bitter are these hours I am going through, these nights I spend in solitude? If any help comes my way, everything will be all right. No matter how ill he is, if I am there to nurse him, he is bound to get well ... Otherwise, bereft and needy as he is, his frail health will deteriorate, and that hereditary disease of his will have the upper hand[52] ...

Tuesday 6th, 11 a.m.

Had a letter from Brieux: I realise that in the literary domain, I have a vast amount of work to do. Am determined to *do it, because I must.*

How strange: as I was writing the above, I felt a slight improvement in my outlook, no doubt because I think I might be able to do that short story for *L'Illustration.*

Thursday 8 August 1901, midnight

After reading Dostoyevsky as I do every day, I suddenly feel a great deal of affection for this tiny room of mine. It looks just like a prison cell and bears no resemblance to the rest of the house.

A room that has been lived in for a long time will absorb some of its occupant's essence, so to speak, and thoughts.

Thursday 15 August 1901, 8.30 p.m.

I have been longing for the desert again these last few days, with an intensity so keen it almost hurts. Just to go as far as old Biskra's last segnia, where Slimène and I stopped that night *six long months ago!*

Oh, to be free right now, the two of us, to be well off and leave for that country which is *ours!* Will I ever set eyes on those magnificent sands again?

To go away and be a tramp again, free and unencumbered as I used to be, even if it means all sorts of new ordeals! To run as fast as my legs will carry me along the Quai de La Joliette – the only part of this town that I love because it is the gate to Africa, and board ship – a humble, unknown figure – and flee, flee at last *for good*!

Friday 16 August, 11 a.m.

Oh, to turn my back on all this and go away for good, now that I am more of an outsider here than in any other place. They do not respect the sacred things I hold so dear, for they are blind and *bourgeois*, bourgeois to their very fingertips, and mired in the base obsessions of their greedy, brutish lives.

Yet they are *quite right* to push me to the limits of my endurance, for that way my heart lets go of them completely. These coarse and nasty scenes of theirs do not affect me any longer. I no longer care and only cling more passionately than ever to the beloved Ideal that is my salvation and my *raison d'être*, and also to Slimène. From his letters I can tell he too has begun to think, a development that is bound to steer him along the same luminous course I am pursuing.

All the pain I feel is due to my being on tenterhooks while waiting for Slimène.

I must stop sacrificing all for the sake of people over here, and start thinking of a home of my *own*.

Reppmann and Brieux[53] have no idea, especially Reppmann, that his largesse has not benefited me and that I did my begging for the sake of others, who simply took it all for granted!

Saturday 17 August

I feel a deep uncertainty about Slimène's transfer. And then there is something else as well. To judge by his last letter, he seems to be thinking of the same thing as I am, namely, the heady subject of physical love. The most delicious and unchaste dreams are visiting me these days. Of course I could not tell anyone about a secret like that, except Dr Taste,[54] a confidant who used to be as brutal as he was sensitive.

There is no doubt about it, I do love Taste … physically the least attractive man I have ever known, at least where the senses are concerned. Not that I did not care for the man's eroticism, the way it would go from the rough and brutal to a form so subtle it would verge on the neurotic. I used to say things to him that no one else has ever heard me say … D.[55] is too down-to-earth and there is something about him that reeks of a tolerance too sweeping and too coarse.

Now that those people are all gone from my present life, I look back with amazement at a figure like Toulat,[56] and wonder if there too there is not some age-old atavism at work: how can the Arab way of life, the *Arab soul* itself, have rubbed off on a Frenchman from Poitiers? Oh yes, Toulat is an Arab all right. He broods, and goes in for harsh and savage living in the desert; of all the French officers I ever knew, he is the only one who is not bored there. His very harshness and his violence are Arabic, in fact. There is something savage too about the way he loves, something un-French and un-modern, for love me he did without a doubt. His love was at its peak the day he wept such desperate tears when we came to Biskra. But he did not understand me and he was afraid of me. He thought the only thing to do was run.

All that does seem so long ago! All the more so as I feel no anger at the thought of any of *them*: the woman who used to think she loved those distant ghosts is now *dead*. The one who is alive today is so different she can no longer answer for past errors.

Sexual matters will continue to hold my attention, of course, from the intellectual point of view, and I would not give up my research in that domain for anything in the world. As far as I am concerned, though, I now have a focus for my sexuality, and the silly phrase: 'I am no longer my own master' is quite to the point. When it comes to the senses, Slimène is my one and only, undisputed master. He is the only one I feel attracted to, the only one to put me in the mood to forget the intellect and descend – is it a descent? I doubt it very much – to the proverbial realm of sexual exploits.

Our modern world is so distorted and so warped that in

marriage the husband is hardly ever the one to do the initiating into sensuality. Stupid and revolting as it is, young girls are hitched to a husband for life, and he is a ridiculous figure in the end. The woman's physical virginity is all his. She is then expected to spend the rest of her life with him, usually in disgust, and suffer what is known as her 'marital duty', until the day that someone comes along to teach her, in a web of lies, the existence of a whole universe of thrills, thoughts and sensations that will regenerate her from head to toe. That is where our marriage is so different from any other – and shocks so many solid citizens: Slimène means two things to me – he is both friend and lover.

Just what did that strange, compelling man, Colonel de R, who held so many first-rate women under his spell, mean when he said: 'You were much sought after in Algeria' ... ? That was something I already knew too well, having found it out at my expense.

None of the men I have known, and that goes for the officers in particular, can understand what Slimène is doing in my life. Domercq had no choice but to accept it in the end. Taste *pretends* he does not understand, but he probably does. What does De R. think of it? I would certainly like to see that man again and get to know him better. He cannot have been an ordinary fellow.

So far I know nothing about Brieux's benevolent personality, except that he must be very kind ... Is he unaffected, like those brief letters of his, simple, open and straightforward, or is he the most complicated of men?

Among the local figures of note, there is that nice man Mohammed ben Aïssa, who must have left for Algiers by now, and has a very kind heart.

Smaïne ben Amma – a man who is rotten to the core. His alcohol intake will lead to either *delirium tremens* or general paralysis.

I could not find him more unpleasant, and there was no need for Zouïzou to put me on my guard against him.

If I had to choose between that 'aristocrat' and the porter who likes his kif, I would definitely choose the latter.

My ordeal is not yet over. Yet if I try to *reason* instead of giving in to instincts, there has actually been a change for the better in my plight: Zouïzou has left that horrible Batna, he is on his way and what is more, he is now in Bône, the city where my mother's grave is. May she make him feel at home, inspire him and take him under her posthumous protection for the rest of his life.

No point in insisting. Augustin is hardly to blame, in fact – except where his weakness is concerned – and that is not all his fault.

He has made a fatal mistake in his marriage and there is nothing anyone can do about it now.

My God, what a relief it would be if Exempliarsky were prepared to lend Augustin enough money to spare us any further expense that might be disastrous!

We have so many debts and needs. Those 25 francs from the old lady would really come in handy. ☾ *May Allah lend a helping hand!*

I must make a huge effort to get through this week without giving in to depression and put the time to good use – which is the hardest part.

The writer I like best right now is Dostoyevsky – perhaps because his novels remind me so much of the diffuse and hazy, troubled outlook that has bedevilled me for so long.

I re-read my friend Eugène's letters last night. My God, how he has changed in the six years that we have been friends! What a difference there is between his first rather green letters and his last ones, after his return from the heart of the desert, from Toulat, a place whose very name is enough to make my imagination soar! What a pall has come over that soul of his! I have the feeling that the romance he had in Algiers had a lot to do with it. The affair in question must have been serious and genuine, to judge by his very despondent letter in which he wrote that he was off for the deep South, almost as if he were on the run.

Had an awful day yesterday, because of yet another pinprick from Augustin's wife.

Kept wandering through town from three to five in the afternoon, tottering on my feet, exhausted and worn out, looking for Smaïne. Did not find him. Went to Joliette, found my friend the porter. Borrowed 55 cents, sent cable to Zouïzou, and bought some tobacco. Went home. Great fatigue, felt ill, pain all over my body.

Saturday 24 August 1901, 10 p.m.

Allah has heard us at long last! After the bad news I had yesterday, the colonel came in person to tell me the transfer is official. Zouïzou will definitely be here in three days' time, and we have the colonel's protection.

Oh how enigmatic human destinies are! How unfathomable the paths where God leads his creatures!

Monday 26 August 11 a.m.

Having felt vaguely unwell these days, I had a curious fit yesterday ... I lay down in the afternoon because I had a bad colic and pain in my lower back. By four o'clock I had a headache that grew sharper by the minute, plus a high fever. I knew I was in a state of delirium, which wore me out.

They simply left me all alone in the house till 10 p.m., without any help whatsoever. When they did come home, they did not even bother to come in and see how I was. Thanks to Allah, though, I have only two more days to go in this horrible existence.

If I do not feel ill tonight, I ought to go and see the room at the hotel, for tomorrow I should go and look for the porter and for Smaïne.

Tuesday 27 August 1901, noon

It has been a long time since I have felt as calm as I do today. The mistral is blowing hard, and it is a lovely autumn day. The air is pure and clear. It is cool outside, the sun is shining and *tomorrow I shall leave this house*.

To put it in a nutshell, I forgive them for everything, and

let Him be the judge. I have done my human duty and will keep doing it for the sake of my dead mother.

Things have simmered down a bit, both in my outward circumstances and within my soul. There still are many questions to be settled, such as that of our marriage, which only raises a problem because we have no money. As we have the colonel's protection, I hope all will be well on that score too.

How many clouds are gone from our horizon! And most importantly, if God does not part us by death, the days of separation are now over *for good*.

27 August, in the evening

We have left Augustin's house.

At four o'clock to Quai de la Joliette. Zouïzou arrived on the *Ville d'Oran* on 28 August 1901 at 8.30 in the morning, lovely clear weather, strong wind . . .

Isabelle takes up her journal again a few days before her marriage.

1 October 1901, 3 p.m.
67, rue Grignan

A month has gone by since I wrote those last lines. It is true that everything has changed. Zouïzou is with me here, and his health is not as bad as I had expected it to be. We are alone and in a *place of our own* – a wonderful feeling! We shall be married in a few days' time and the *Villa* has been sold.

Poor dear *Villa Neuve*, I know I will never set foot in it again.

Ever since I found out yesterday that *the house* was sold on 27 September I have been haunted by memories of it.

That means the end, for good this time, of the story of my life there, the first life I had on earth! Everything has been dispersed, it all lies buried or is gone. In a few days' time even the old furniture, inanimate witness of our past, will be auctioned off and scattered.

God has had mercy on me and granted me my prayer:

He has given me the ideal companion, the one I had longed for with such ardour. Without him, my life would always have remained all gloom and incoherence.

For the moment we are having a hard and penniless time, but then again, ✝ *he who suffers till the very end will be the only one to find salvation.*

God knows what He has in mind for us. That means we must resign ourselves and have courage in the face of adversity, in the firm conviction that life on earth is but a phase along the way to other, unknown destinies.

It has been a year already since that luminous, melancholy autumn in the Souf ... The palm trees over there are shaking their shroud of dust by now, the sky is clear and limpid above the splendid dunes.

Meanwhile we are here in this dreary city full of gloom and boredom!

Marseilles, 21 November 1901, 8 p.m.

For several days now, the two of us have been full of sadness, and I am getting a premonition that we are about to leave. ☾ *God knows!*

Memories of the Souf make for an obsession that is thrill and torment all at once. I only need to hear the sound of bugles for a thousand feelings to start stirring in my heart.

Those are the same thoughts I used to have about the netherworld, when I would stand by the window in my room and daydream in the silence of the night, looking at the vast sky above the Jura's jagged, often snow-clad outline, and the black and heavy mass of great trees.

In the springtime there were always countless nightingales in the lilac bushes full of dew. A mysterious sadness would come over me as I listened to them warble. Particularly in childhood, my mind always found strange associations in memories and feelings.

It all comes back to me now, in the insecurity and sheer monotony of my present life.

For the first time since my beloved parents died, I am beginning to *exteriorise* a bit; I now have a duty to fulfil *outside myself*. That alone enhances the days I spend here, for they would otherwise lack meaning; the same goes for the five long months devoid of charm I have spent as an outcast in this city where I have no ties, where everything seems so alien and abhorrent.

How it rankles the common man to see anyone – and a woman at that – depart from the norm and be *herself*!

I am finding out these days that I have a talent I did not know I had for writing essays on such topics as history that are not without a certain depth.

Now more than ever do I realise that I shall never be content with a sedentary life, and that I shall always be haunted by thoughts of a sun-drenched *elsewhere*. The only place where I could end my days would be El Oued.

26 November 1901, 1 a.m.

Feeling calm and sad today, longing to leave, to flee this room, this city and everybody in it.

I feel more and more that these must be the last few days of our exile ... May God make it come true, for the nightmare of our Marseilles days has lasted long enough!

What makes me very happy is that Ouiha is now getting closer to the arcane world of thoughts and feelings, so that I am no longer on my own there.

It is clear that he is the companion I was always meant to have, and how unfathomable is the enigma that surrounds our lives on earth: we lived far apart from each other for ten, twenty, twenty-five years without either of us having the slightest inkling of the other's existence, yet we were both in search of the *one and only* partner, the one without whom there could be no happiness on earth.

The curious thing is that on 19 June, 1900, I had the first hint of the sort of life that I might lead. It happened in the grim and dirty room I had at Madame Pons's. I was writing a chapter of *Rakhil*, when the notion of *going to Ouargla* came to me out of the blue! That thought of mine was the beginning of it all!

Oh, if at every moment of our lives we could know the consequences of some of the utterings, thoughts and deeds that seem so trivial and unimportant at the time! And should we not conclude from such examples that there is no such thing in life as unimportant moments devoid of meaning for the future?

85

To change the subject altogether: As I go over the history of Carthage with Ouïha, I am struck by the resemblance of the callous Carthage of antiquity to present-day England: their greed, their contempt for anything foreign, their boundless, intransigent egotism ... Might those traits be characteristic of all great *maritime* powers?

To broaden my vision further, I would need to make a serious study of history. Grocery bills and tailor's invoices are taking up the precious time, alas, that I would like to devote to thought!

Saturday 30 November 1901, 3 p.m.

It is freezing cold and all we have to keep warm with is the wood M. gives us, but he has an *ulterior motive* ... ☾
May Allah's curse come down on all those who do wrong, as Slimène puts it.

What will be the outcome of our present mess?

If we manage to settle our worst debts and if my friend Eugène sends me another hundred francs, we will of course leave for Bône on the spot and stay there for an indefinite length of time. When will we be able to head for Algiers? God only knows!

Yet despite all the trouble, the physical and emotional strain, there is one thing that delights me: Zouïzou's soul is constantly growing closer to mine. I have found the partner of my dreams at last. May he live as long as my life on earth lasts!

A thick dark fog of conjecture and uncertainty is all around us. Yet there is one ray of hope, and that is that we may soon be on our way home to the country of our choice, probably to stay there for good.

Before we do, there will be one sad, quick and almost stealthy visit to Geneva.[57]

Isabelle and Slimène finally return to Algeria.

Bône, Tuesday 21 January 1902

Sailed from Marseilles on 14 January at 5 p.m. on the *Duc de Bragance*. Reached Bône on the 15th at eight o'clock in the evening.

Our dream of going home from exile has come true at last; we are back on the soil where the sun is always young, our beloved land facing the great blue murmuring sea whose vast empty stretches make one think of the Sahara's.

May this year mark the beginning of a turn in our lives, with the serenity we have yearned for and deserve as our reward!

Bône, Wednesday 29 January 11 a.m.

Outdoor living and the simplicity of life down here are beginning to restore my strength. I had none left at the end of that long and painful period of exile in Marseilles. What is more, my brain is stirring too, and I think I may do some writing here.

Twenty-one days from now, Zouïzou will also be free of his obligations to the army, so that he will have far more freedom and will no longer need to be wary of indiscretions. We will then have to manage by ourselves in this vast, magnificent universe that has its lures and disappointments.

The brief span of time I must spend on earth does not frighten me; the only thing that does is the thought that I might lose my partner and be left all by myself.

As for my morale, *almost* total resignation and equanimity, which, as I have said before, all has a good deal to do with physical factors. I don't wish to have anything to do with the world at large and be a city-dweller once again: I am thrilled to be a hermit.

When the two of us went by ourselves the other night to meet Ali Bou Traïf on the Pont de la Casbah, we saw the full moon rise over the tranquil sea. We stopped at the turn in the road that goes to the cemetery.

The bridge looked like the mystical one of the Slavic legend, the one that is woven for nymphs out of moonbeams in the silence of the night. All golden, it trembled slightly against the waters' shifting background. A strip of grey cloud came between moon and water, so that its shadow could be seen there, the shape of a low dune with two promontories dividing the sea in two halves, one very blue, vast and bright, the other a dull misty grey melting

87

into the horizon. In that one there was a fishing boat with a Latin sail. There was no reflection of it on the waters' misty surface; it was not moving, but seemed like a phantom vessel that vanished slowly into the fog.

14 February 1902, 3 p.m.

A month has gone by since we left that inferno in Marseilles and everything has gone awry already over here because of the constant intrigues of these Moorish women.

Here, as elsewhere, I can see how volatile Slimène's character is, and what a bad influence his environment has on him. Will that change some day? I do not know, and in any case, a temperament such as his can do nothing to alleviate the poverty to which we are now reduced.

Far better to start another life of poverty over in Algiers – which would in any event be less dreadful than in Marseilles – than stay here, where hospitality takes the form of constant snubs and endless arguments.

My literary bent is stirring, and I shall try to make a name for myself in the Algerian press at least, while waiting for the opportunity to do the same in Paris.

To do all that I would have to have total peace and quiet for a while, almost to the point of seclusion. I would have to find someone in Algiers to teach Slimène all the things he does not know, which is a tall order, and that would take a lot of worries off my hands and leave me free to work. ☾ *Allah will see to it!*

I shall go and say one more goodbye to the white grave on its green hill basking in the exuberance of spring, and after that we will be on the road again and lead our lives according to the whims of fate.

Left for Algiers by a coach of the Messageries du Sud on 12 March 1902, at 6.15 in the morning. The weather was bright and clear. Mental outlook – good, peaceful. The journey up the slopes of the Sahel was long and laborious. Birmandreis, Birkadem, Birtouta. Boufarik, Beni-Mered. Reached Blida by half-past noon, went to the café on the Place d'Armes. Had lunch at the station, left again by the coach for Medeah. Sidi-Medani, the Gorges. Ruisseau des Singes, hotel, magnificent torrent, narrow gorge. All along the road countless waterfalls that vanish underground. Thickets of viburnum in bloom and masses of ferns everywhere.

Reached Medeah by 8.30 p.m. Visit to Moorish café. Sent cable to Ouïha. Spent some time sitting on a bench in the square, and then in the café-restaurant at the station. Took the train coming from Maison-Carrée. Reached Algiers by 9.35 in the evening on Friday 14 March.

☾ *Allah does not put the majority of fools on the right course!*

Isabelle meets Victor Barrucand, the journalist and editor.

30 March 1902

Present situation: no money. We rely on Si Muhammad Sherif to come to our rescue and take care of us during these last few days. During the day, I work.

Last Thursday went to see Barrucand at the Villa Bellevue; had a pleasant impression.[58] A modern mind, subtle and perceptive, but biased by the notions of his time. Went to rue du Rempart Médée to Mme Ben-Aben's workshop. Enjoyed my conversation with intellectuals, something I had not experienced in a long time.

A generous man will record the harm done to him in pencil, the good in ink.

'*Behave in this world as if you were to live for ever, and act as if you were to die tomorrow!*' to be compared with Marcus Aurelius's thought on the subject [*Meditations*].

1 April 1902, 9 p.m.

We are still hard at work. We have so little time left – so little! – and so much studying to do to catch up that we cannot stand it. It all takes a huge effort these days. The trouble is, there are so many subjects. Well, ☾ *Allah will help!*

For the moment, I must continue to muster courage enough for two, and when things are really bad, cheer up Zouïzou and restore his optimism, for without that we have no hope at all.

I think it is impossible for human minds to think of Death as a final, irrevocable end to life. As for myself, I have a *conviction* that *eternity* does exist.

Yet ☽ *may Allah the Great forgive me*, if Death did really mean the end of everything, that would not be so bad. Does not, after all, three-quarters of all suffering lie in the memory we have of it, which is to say, in our *awareness* of it?

> *Algiers, 22 April 1902*
> *17, rue du Soudan*

For once, we do not have too much work tonight. I have a moment to myself and after doing some translating for dear, kind Mme Ben-Aben, I have been reading Nadson.

Along the distant shores of the Rhône at the foot of the snow-clad Jura mountains, spring must be about to stir. The trees are covered in a mist of foliage, and the first rock-plants are blooming at the *Villa Neuve* in the shadow of the great pine tree and by the two graves in the Vernier cemetery.

Things are no different this spring from any other year, and Nature is doing what it always does ... The difference is that I am no longer there to do my dreaming and my grieving ... Vava, Maman and Volod have departed for the great Unknown! ... Everything is gone, finished and destroyed.

> *Algiers, 4 May 1902, about 10 p.m.*

Went to see a sorcerer today, who lives in a tiny place in a street in the upper town, via dark stairways in the Rue du Diable. I now have absolute proof that the mysterious science of Magic does actually exist. How vast are the perspectives such knowledge opens up for me, and also what a relief there is in the blow dealt to my doubts!

I am in a calm and wistful mood these days. Algiers is clearly one of those cities which fire my imagination, and certain parts of it in particular. I like the area we are living in, and our lodgings too, after that horrible dump in the rue de la Marine.

How can all those fools in social and literary circles say there is nothing Arab about Algiers?

There is for instance that lovely moment of the maghreb over the harbour and rooftops of the upper town. The place teems with merry Algerian women, all frolicking happily in their pink or green garb against the bluish-white of the rooftops. I see them from the little moucharabieh window at Mme Ben-Aben's.

Together with the one at Bône, the bay of Algiers is one of the prettiest and most captivating seascapes I have ever seen.

Despite the riff-raff French civilisation has brought over here, whore and whoremaster that it is, Algiers is still a place full of grace and charm.

The more I study the history of North Africa – very poorly and too fast – the more I see that I was right: the African soil devours and absorbs all that is hostile to it. It may well be the land where the light is destined to shine forth one day and regenerate the world!

An old man once turned up at the French encampment after the 1830 landing in Sidi-Ferruch. He had a pacific manner, and all he had to say was: 'There is no god but God and Muhammad is his Prophet!' With that he left and was never seen again.

No one understood what he meant by that. He had come to say that Islam and the mesmerising soil of Africa are one for all eternity!

8 June 1902, 11.30 p.m.

Life goes on, monotonous as ever, yet there is the hint of some future direction in the midst of all this dreadful emotional turmoil.

I am going through another slow period of gestation which can be quite painful at times.

The two people who have been helpful to us here, Barrucand and Mme Ben-Aben, are both kind and thoughtful and I am beginning to understand what makes them tick.

Barrucand is a dilettante in the domain of thought and even more so when it comes to feeling, a spiritual nihilist in

91

other words. From a practical standpoint, though, he is someone very positive who knows how to handle himself.

As for Mme Ben-Aben, after my mother, she is the only woman I have met who is both good and enamoured with an ideal, although quite ignorant of 'real life'. Even I, who am totally *inept* at handling myself, know better than they do.

Augustin is now gone from my life; as far as I am concerned the brother I used to love so much is dead. That shadow of him in Marseilles who is married to Jenny the work-horse does not exist for me, and I very rarely think of him.

Now that the torrid heat of summer has suddenly come again, the notion that I am back in Africa is slowly sinking in. Soon I will feel completely at home, especially if my plan to go to Bou-Saada comes off ... Oh, that journey! it will mean a brief return, not to the magnificent Sahara itself, but to a place nearby that has all the palm trees and sunshine one would want!

Remarks about Algiers
While the weather was cool, the shadows in the upper town's dark streets were grey and dark, to the point of gloominess. Now that there is a sudden sharp contrast between light and dark, it all looks African again, or Arab in any event.

No, the true African landscape is not to be found in any of the large cities, certainly not in those of the Tell. African perspectives are hazy with a distant horizon. Vast space and emptiness, a blinding light, are what makes a landscape African! The architecture of Algiers boasts none of those traits. Its houses are all piled on top of each other and huddle fearfully at the bottom of culs-de-sac, in a city accustomed to raids and sieges.

The mindless noise of the crowds, where the only Arabs are those awful Kabyles in European garb, makes certain parts of town look like places of ill repute where no one's life is safe.

The uninitiated European thinks those men in dirty burnouses over tattered European clothes, and those Moorish women are all part of the local colour. But that is precisely what is so un-Arabic about Algiers, for it is contrary to Arab custom. The truth is that Old Algiers is medieval, Turkish, Moorish, or what have you, but not Arabic and certainly not African![59]

In truly Arabic towns like the Ksours in the south, the magic of Africa and its poignant mystery are actually tangible. They lie in the wide open space, the small, low, tumbledown houses, either very white or in the same hue as their hazy environment, in all that light and bleakness.

The trouble with Algiers is its abject population. Any sort of contemplative streetlife, of the calm and fertile, gratifying sort I love so much, is out of the question there.

The savage hatred I feel for crowds is getting worse, natural enemies that they are of imagination and of thought. They make it impossible for me to feel *alive* here, the way I do in other places. Oh, how evil civilisation is! Why was it ever brought over here?

M'sila, 29 June 1902, 2 p.m.

I left Algiers yesterday, 28 June, at 7.50 in the morning. The weather looked ominous and cloudy ... There were almost no stops, and the journey went by in a flash, as in a dream.

I am in a tiny hotel room, where I am waiting for supper. The heat is stifling. There has been a sirocco ever since we passed the Portes-de-Fer, and the countryside looks like a steambath. The sky is misty in that incandescent way brought on by thunder.

The road from Bou-Arreridj to M'sila goes through solitary places; some of them are parched, others marshy. Here and there runs a winding valley, lined with oleanders in bloom, its smell an acrid one of humidity.

From Medjez to M'sila, slept any way I could on top of a crate. Reached our destination by three in the morning. Went to the Moorish café, and to the market with Fredj. Had lunch inside the mosque, where it was cool and dark and there were relatively few flies. After that I came here for the siesta.

As always, it all feels like a dream, this journey, and sudden separation from Ouïha ... Poor Ouïha, who is without a penny and has got to cope with the ever worsening tedium of Algiers! If I could at least bring him some relief with this journey of mine!

I shall now try to go back to sleep, so that I will not be worn out during the night.

Bou-Saada, 1 July 1902

After a morning spent on clarifications with the Sid-el-Hokkaïn, we spent the afternoon in a garden belonging to the zawyia.

M'sila is a town built of mud, and it is divided in two by a deep oued. The greyish-brown houses have the dilapidated look of the Ksour, an impression that is reinforced by the handful of palm trees.

It was the maghreb hour, and I went by myself to wait for Si Embarek near the mosque located by the oued's edge. The sun was setting in the sort of mist that always comes with the sirocco. On the other side of the oued stood the old part of town; its curiously shaped marabout shrines and its sombre gardens all gave it a decidedly Saharan air. Tahar Djadi's mare is an excellent horse and I could not resist the temptation to let her run a bit. I felt as if I were back in the old days, when I had peace and freedom. We reached the borj of the Tolbas after dark, a solitary edifice, square and sombre in its desert setting. Had a second supper outdoors by the wall.

Had a bad night inside the courtyard, where I was devoured by fleas. When I saw the moon in its last quarter come up, pale and drenched in mist, I woke up the talebs and we left. We took a number of Arab shortcuts, via Saïda and Baniou. All we saw of Saïda in the early morning darkness were the black outlines of houses built of mud, without so much as a tree or garden, a grim sight indeed in the midst of that desert.

Farther on, while the taleb were saying the fajr prayer, I stretched out on the ground at the westernmost point. Si Ali, the talba, then left us, astride the red mare whose graceful little bay foal trotted alongside.

We continued on our way by ourselves. Baniou, a borj built high up, and a handful of houses made of toub. An alleyway lined with poplar trees.

94

Had coffee thick with flies and a drink of muddy water, in the shadow of some tamarind trees growing in yellowish sand.

In the sebkha before Baniou I felt so exhausted by the grey mare I had taken in the borj of the Tolbas that I dismounted and went barefoot for quite some time.

After Banou, we stopped at Bir-el-Hali: dilapidated houses made of toub, a well with good water. It was getting hotter and I continued my journey by mule. Drank along the way from a camel-driver's guerba.

Caught sight of Bou-Saada among the bluish mountains, with its casbah set on top of a rock, and a handful of very low, small dunes that looked white in the distance.

Arrival in Bou-Saada. On one side of it are spacious gardens enclosed by walls of toub. In the river bed stand oleanders in full bloom. On the high ground on the other side stand the town's houses. It is a picturesque and hilly place intersected by lush ravines where, among the dark green of the fig trees and vineyards, the odd oleander strikes a bright pink note and the pomegranate trees in bloom, vivid scarlet ones.

The heat was torrid yesterday thanks to the sirocco, and culminated in a violent storm last night. It does give the place that beloved and familiar atmosphere. Bou-Saada is surrounded by tall and arid, reddish-looking hills that block the horizon from view.

We dismounted under the arcade of the sheikh's house, near the justice of the peace. Facing it lies a scrawny, walled-in French garden. To the left stands a munitions depot and an unkempt garden where frogs croak all night long. The population is obsequious toward the 'hakkam', and a good deal more coarse and harsh than people in the Sahara.

Despite yesterday's heavy rainfall, the ground is parched. There are beautiful, slender-limbed camels of a Saharan breed that come to kneel down in front of the sheikh's house.

This afternoon we will set off for El-Hamel ... When will I be going home? When will I be seeing Zouïzou? Those are questions to which I do not know the answers.

The official tree here is a very green sort of mulberry, as

well as a variety of acacia whose flowers are like tiny yellow balls.

In any event, the journey alone has made it worth my while to come and discover this place which is, after all, part of my beloved South. In my present circumstances, this fairly long journey has been a golden opportunity.

The women's costume is unbecoming, in particular the huge flat headgear. Unless the Southern women's costume is worn by graceful, tall, slim women, it is dreadful. The one worn in the Souf is prettier and has more style. I cannot say anything about the women's physique, for I have not seen any. The little girls are heavily tattooed and have pale and savage faces.

El-Hamel, 2 July 1902, during the siesta hour

After the Moorish bath last night, we heard that Lella Zainab[60] had returned to the zawyia, but the darkness of the night, the wind and rain all kept us from setting out. Slept underneath the arcade.

Woke up very early. Talked with Sidi Embarek[61] till daybreak, and set off together without any coffee, he by mule, I on a handsome young white horse.

Slimène, Isabelle's husband, was named Khoja, or secretary to the administration of Ténès.

Ténès, 7 July 1902

My journey to Bou-Saada went so fast it felt like a dream, and I came back feeling all the stronger for it and cured of the morbid indolence that had been plaguing me in Algiers ... my soul too has begun to stir again. A nomad I was even when I was very small and would stare at the road, that white spellbinding road headed straight for the unknown ... a nomad I will remain for life, in love with distant and uncharted places.

Orléansville, 17 July 1902, 9.15 p.m.

Here I am again, back on the road, headed for Algiers. Luckily I will only be there for a few days on business for the zawyia and Mme Ben-Aben. After that I will go back to Ténès, for a long time to come.

I left Ténès at six in the morning, in lovely clear weather. I was feeling tired and sleepy. When I got to the Trois Palmiers, I found the local policeman and a good horse. Went to see the caïd, whose name is Ahmed. The house stands on top of a high hill where the view is very beautiful: the African landscape's arid slopes follow each other in a variety of colours all the way into the very luminous distance. Set off again on horseback. Reached Orléansville by about six o'clock. It clearly is one of the prettiest cities in the interior, especially because of its setting. On its northern side it has a very high view of the Cheliff, and is surrounded by lush gardens.

I have been having a severe bout of fever ever since I got here, and I more or less lost consciousness for a few moments ... I am finding it difficult to write. I pray that I will not fall ill in Algiers, so far from my poor beloved Zouïzou!

Ténès, 25 August, evening

I am sitting on an arid hill facing the valley and the chaotic mass of slopes and mountains drenched in mist. The tall mountains along the horizon stand out in grey against the reddish-orange of the setting sun. All is peaceful in this Bedouin country, even though there may be the odd vague sound, the barking of dogs and the shouts of men.

To the right, beyond the gorges, lies a hazy stretch of sea, to judge by the empty horizon. To the left, at the top of a pointed hill, a dense thicket of shrubs which hide a handful of blackish stones that constitute a shrine, the grave of a marabout. Night is falling and all sounds are dying.

Ténès, Thursday 18 September 1902, 9 a.m.

The autumn has come. There has been a strong wind on quite a few occasions, and the sky is overcast with grey clouds. Our life is as monotonous as always, which would not be so bad if it were not for the perennial money problems. Yet here we do at least have the security of being able to satisfy our basic needs.

The problem with Ténès is its herd of neurotic, orgiastic, mean and futile females. Needless to say, here as elsewhere, mediocre people cannot abide me. All their mud leaves me cold, however, except when it comes too close for comfort.[62]

I have visited many places here, the Maïn, the Baghdoura, Tarzout, Cape Kalax, the M'guen ... Up and down the countryside I have been, through peaceful Bedouin territory whose boundaries are still so vast.

As for my mental outlook, these last few days have been bleak, and strangely enough, as usually happens nowadays, Ouïha is feeling the same way too. I am worried about his health. It may be, of course, that with regular treatment he will get better once and for all. If he was named caïd and if we went away from all the idiocy in Ténès, to some place in the mountains where the air is pure, with lots of rest and healthy living, he would certainly be happy.

As far as my literary activities go, these last few days have been a total loss. Today I am beginning to feel better, and this evening I will no doubt leave for the big annual feast at Sidi Merouan. My report on those festivities can give me the material for my next article for the ungrateful *Nouvelles*. The location and subject are just right for it. These last few days my health has been letting me down again. Is it the effect of my body on my mind, or vice versa?

Maïn, 21 September 1902, 10 p.m.

Once again I am the butt of the Algerian administration's boundless stupidity: the Commissioner has had a letter from Algiers. What will they think of next? The fact is, that the little folk in Ténès have turned in a report.

I am here in Maïn, in a small, clean room. The only drawback is that outside the window the billy goat keeps bleating and leaping about with female goats. Perhaps he will go to sleep at last ...

I came here by myself, in clear, very windy weather.

What is so strange and, on the surface at least, in total contradiction with the natives' character, is that the educated ones will confide in a woman like myself at the drop of a hat and talk to her in a way they certainly would not talk to any man; witness the conversation I had with Si Elbedrani by the side of the road in the clear blue light just before dawn ...

Maïn, 22 September, 2 p.m.

I am all alone, in this small room of mine; the weariness of the last few days has *suddenly* evaporated and given way to a fruitful melancholia.

I have re-read my earlier diaries. No doubt about it, my present life is sheer bliss compared to that of recent years, even the Geneva ones! And as for any comparison between now and the time I spent in Marseilles!

There is a silence here that feels eternal. I should like to come and live here [or some place like it] for months on end, to shield my eyes from the ugliness of European humanity, for I loathe it more and more.

The only person in Ténès I like to talk to is my friend Arnaud.[63] But then, he himself gets no respect from that bunch of pretentious Philistines who strut about sporting tight trousers and silly hats.

Whatever their unenlightened way of life, the lowliest of Bedouins are far superior to those idiotic Europeans making such a nuisance of themselves.

Where can one go to flee them, where can one go to live far away from those arrogant, prying, evil beings who fashion everything in their own dreadful image?

I shall write to Nablus and look into the possibility of settling in Palestine, once I come into the ✝ *White Spirit*'s money, which will no doubt be soon.

Flee Europe, even in its transplanted form, go to some Arab country, similar no doubt to the one I love, and start a whole new life there ... Perhaps that will still happen! ☽ *Allah knows the things that are hidden and the measure of people's sincerity.*

Ténès, 26 September 1902, 9 p.m.

The year has almost run its course, and so has this notebook. Where will we be a year from now, at the start of the rainy season when the countryside dons its pale shroud and takes its yearly rest, when asphodels bloom by winding roads? Neither of us thinks we will be here for very long. What ultimate direction will our destinies take?

It is cold and rainy. I worry about Ouïha's health in such bad weather.

It will not be long before my journey to Bou-Saada. Another visit to the South, its date palms, sandy wastes and grey horizons.

Algiers, Wednesday 13 October 1902, 5 p.m.

I have been here for ten days now, far from those peaceful lodgings of mine and from my sweet companion ... I am feeling sad, in the way that always produces ideas. Curiously enough, I am beginning to get a better notion of this part of the country and savour its special splendour.

The great bay of Algiers is as smooth as a mirror. The opposite shore looks violet with its pink houses ... Here on Mustapha's hill all is peaceful.

I may have to go to France this winter to see about writing a piece in defence of the Marguerite rebels.[64] Oh! if I could only say everything I know, speak my mind and come out with the whole truth! What a good deed that would be! In due course it would have positive results and establish my reputation too! Brieux was certainly right about that: I must start my career by coming out openly in defence of my Algerian Muslim brethren.[65]

I must stay here for at least a week. After that I shall have a great deal of work, for I shall have to do the brochure, probably write an article a week for *La Dépêche*, and little by little collect enough short stories to make a book and have them ready for the day my name will mean something in Paris, after the Margueritte trial. I shall be taking a big step this winter toward peace and salvation, so that my Ouïha and I will feel more serene at last.

Oh, Mama! Oh, Vava! Look at your child, who has followed in your footsteps and honoured you beyond the grave! I am not forgetting you. I shall always remember you. When things were at their worst, it was to you I turned.

The weather was beautifully clear Friday morning when I set out for the boundary of Oran province. Until the Bou-Zraya marketplace I had Lakhdar ben Ziou for a companion, a sombre and most unrewarding individual. At one point the road goes by the foot of a hill that is overshadowed by a sharp cliff. The cliff's soil is a beautiful and warm reddish-brown. There is a brief glimpse of Fromentin in the distance in between two mountains, or rather two high hills. It is a recently built village full of eucalyptus trees, a place without character, like all those villages built on lands taken from poor peasants who now work there on the ruthless terms set by the French Khammesat. The peasants do complain, but they bear their lot with utmost patience. For how long though?

The caïd of the Beni-Merzoug lives on a low slope below a hill called Mekamat al-Murabtine, so named after the Murabtine, a clan whose women are almost all prostitutes about whom the strangest witchcraft stories are told.

We could not find the caïd; so his son and I went back to Fromentin, where I was given a guide who was an idiot by the name of Djellouli Bou Khaled. We started out and kept wandering aimlessly. He did not know his way around.

The next afternoon we went to see the Ouled-Belkassem clan, an hour and fifteen minutes away. They live in a borj and mechta surrounded by a thornbush hedge, in a magnificent site. The regal-looking Ouarsenis Mountains[66] towered above the entire expanse of the Shelif plain. To the left, Orléansville looked like an oasis full of black greenery. To the right, the first plains of the Oran region stretched out as far as the eye could see.

The reason for our going there was a sad one, and apart from the admirable panorama I saw, the memory I have of that lap of my journey is a grim one, for we went to see a little girl who had been burned alive in curious circumstances that will never be explained.

Everything is very peaceful in this remote part of the world, very far from any contact with Europeans, a place where it is still possible to find repose.

Have good memories of that long trip. I suddenly had

101

another brainstorm, and think it was a useful one. I was travelling slowly in the sunshine along the road between Baghdoura and Fromentin, munching on a deliciously crisp cake I had bought in the market and on some dried figs I had been given by my travelling companion. Write a novel, tell the unique story of a man – rather like myself – who is a Muslim and tries to sow the seeds of virtue everywhere he goes. I must still find the plot, which would have to be simple and striking.

Today was the beginning of Ramadan,[67] a very special time of year, rife with strange emotions and, in my case, with wistful recollections. This is the third since the destinies of Ouïha and myself were joined. For the moment our life is peaceful and free of any immediate worries. ☾ *'Praise to Allah for delivering us!'*

Algiers, 25 December 1902

My discontent with people grows by leaps and bounds ... dissatisfaction with myself as well, for I have not managed to find a suitable *modus vivendi*, and am beginning to fear that none is possible with my temperament.

There is only one thing that can help me get through the years I have on earth, and that is writing. It has the huge advantage of giving the will a free hand, without making us have to cope with the world out there. That in itself is vital, whatever else it may yield in the way of career or gain, especially as I am more and more convinced that life as such is hostile and a dead end.

As of now, I will probably go to Medeah and Bou-Saada once the last five days of Ramadan are over.

Once again my soul is caught in a period of transition, undergoing changes and, no doubt, growing darker still and more oppressed. If this foray of mine into the world of darkness does not stop, what will be its terrifying outcome?

Yet I do believe there is a remedy, but in all heartfelt humility ☾ *it lies in the realm of the Islamic religion.*

That is where I shall find peace at last, and solace for my heart. The impure and, so to speak, hybrid atmosphere I now live in does me no good. My soul is withering and turns inward for its distressing observations.

As agreed, I set off for the Dahra on the evening of Thursday 11 December by the light of the Ramadan moon.

The night was clear and cool. There was total silence all over that desert town, as rider Muhammad and I slipped through like shadows. That man is so much a Bedouin and so close to nature that he is my favourite companion, for he is in total harmony with the landscape and the people ... not to mention my own frame of mind. He is not aware of it, but he is as preoccupied as I am with the puzzle and enigma of the senses.

At Montenotte and Cavaignac we went to the Moorish cafés there. We crossed oueds, went up slopes and down ravines, past graveyards ...

In a desert full of diss and doum, above a grim-looking shelf rather like those in the Sahara with shrubs perched high up on mounds, we dismounted to eat and to get some rest. The place felt so unsafe we started at the slightest noise. I spotted a vague white silhouette against one of the shrubs down below. The horses snorted restlessly ... who was it? The shadow vanished, and when we went by that spot, the horses were uneasy.

Our path led through a narrow valley intersected by many oueds. Jackals howled near by. Farther down we came to the mechta of Kaddour-bel-Korchi, the caïd of the Talassa.

The caïd was not there and we had to go farther still, until we found him in the mechta of a certain Abd-el-Kader ben Aïssa, a pleasant, hospitable man. We had our meal there and once the moon had set, we went off for Baach by paths that were riddled with holes and full of mud and rolling stones. At dawn the borj of Baach, the most beautiful in the area, came into sight high up on a pointed hill, looking very similar to a borj in the Sahara ...

Algiers, 29 December 1902, 2.30 a.m.

How curious and dreamlike is my impression – is it a pleasant one? I can't tell! – of life in Algiers, with all the weariness that goes with the end of Ramadan!

Ramadan! We spent its first few days in Ténès, in the soothing climate of family life the way it is at that time of year. What a curious family we are, made up of people who have drifted together by accident, Slimène and I, Bel-Hadj from Bou-Saada, and Muhammad, who has one foot in the unforgettable Souf and another on those poetic slopes overlooking the blue bay and road to Mostaganem ...

31 December 1902, midnight

Another year has slipped by ... One year less to live ... I love life, out of curiosity and for the pleasure of discovering its mysteries.

Even when I was tiny, I used to think with terror of the time when our beloved elders would have to die. It seemed to me impossible they would! Five years have now gone by since Mama was laid to rest in a graveyard on Islamic soil ... It will soon be four years ago that Vava was buried in Vernier over in the land of exile, next to Volodia whose death has never been explained. ...

And everything else is gone. That fateful, hapless house has passed into other hands ... Augustin has vanished from my horizon where he used to loom so large. I have been roaming in anguish by myself, my only companion the man I found in the Souf, long may he stay at my side and bring me solace, ☽ *please Allah.*

What will next year bring us? What new hopes and disappointments? Despite so many changes, it is good to have a loving heart to call one's own, and friendly arms in which to rest.

Algiers, Sunday 9 January 1903,
midnight

It would be nice to die in Algiers, facing the harmony of that vast bay with the jagged profile of the Kabyle mountains in the distance.

Who knows how long my stay in Algiers will last, who knows how it will end? Who knows where I shall be tomorrow? Another journey southwards, in the direction of the desert, land where the sun is fiery and the palm trees' shadows blue upon the soil.

What I would like right now is to live over in Ténès, lead a quiet life there free of shackles, and keep going off on horseback in pursuit of my dream, from tribe to tribe.

Isabelle, after a series of short restless trips, journeys to Bou-Saada to visit the maraboute Lella Zainab.

Bou-Saada, Wednesday 28 January 1903, half past noon

Left Algiers at six o'clock on Monday 26th in clear weather. Reached Bou-Saada at 7.30 in the evening, stayed at the Moorish bath. Never have I been so keenly aware here of the vaguely ominous weight that seems to hang over all the occupied territories; it is something one cannot put one's finger on, but there are so many ambiguities and innuendoes, so many mysteries . . .

In spite of my fatigue, and lack of sleep and food, this has been a good journey. The Ziar are kind and simple people, who sang their saint's *medha* to the accompaniment of gasba, zorna and bendar, each in turn, while the train wended its way in the sunshine I was so happy to have found again.

Chellal is a dreary village built of toub, a handful of wretched cottages set in a hollow full of water. An acrid smell of iodine and saltpetre hangs in the air.

The native population is made up of Ouled-Madhi and of Hachem, who are not very congenial. The maghreb was superb, with the mountains standing out in bluish-black against the reddish-gold of the sky.

I visited the Arab Bureau this morning, and by about one o'clock I went for a stroll in the Arab part of town, and in the oued, where Arab washerwomen stood out in blue and red dots of an incredibly warm intensity.

Once I rest tomorrow night at El-Hamel, I will do a better job of writing down my observations. The physical fatigue and lack of food I suffered till tonight have worn me out. The ride to El-Hamel will be good training for the long journey to Sahari and Boghar.

It looks as if I am no longer being persecuted. They tell me there had been no advance word of my arrival, yet they have been most pleasant, even the commanding officer . . . how shadowy and mysterious these people are!

105

There is a heavy silence all around, and the only sound to break it is the occasional noise coming from the village or the zawyia, the distant sound of dogs barking and the raucous growls of camels.

El-Hamel! How appropriate that name is for this corner of old Islam, so lost in these barren mountains and so veiled in unfathomable mystery.

The same evening, about 10 o'clock

I am sitting on my bed, near the fireplace in the vaulted main room. That cheerful-looking fire and my bed right on the floor make the room look so much more gay and cosy than it did earlier in the day.

The 'hotel', a large square edifice, boasts a deep and desolate-looking inner courtyard full of bricks and stones. It leads to the upper floor which is divided into two rooms, a small and a large one, both of them with semicircular vaults, like well-to-do houses in the Souf. One of the windows looks out over the cemeteries in a south-western direction, the three others give out on to the east. There are three French beds, an oval table, chairs, all set on very thick rugs. With a few more authentically Arab touches, the room would look truly grand. I wish I could arrange it myself and do it justice. On the western side stand the tall buildings made of toub where the maraboute lives. To the north is the new mosque with its great round cupola surrounded by smaller ones, and inside it stands the tomb of Sidi Muhammad Belkassem.

I am going to lie down and rest, for tomorrow I must rise early to go and see the maraboute. No doubt I will return to Bou-Saada tomorrow afternoon, and will try to be there by the maghreb. After that I will have a week for a good look and that is a time I must not waste.

Bou-Saada, Saturday 31 January, 1 p.m.

We arrived here from El-Hamel yesterday at three in the afternoon.

Every time I see Lella Zainab I feel rejuvenated, happy for no tangible reason and reassured. I saw her twice yesterday in the course of the morning. She was very good and very kind to me, and was happy to see me again.

Visited the tomb of Sidi Muhammad Belkassem, very small and simple in that large mosque, which will be very beautiful by the time it is finished. I then went to pray on the hillside facing the grave of El-Hamel's pilgrim founders.

I did some galloping along the road, together with Si Bel-Abbès, under the paternal gaze of Si Ahmed Mokrani. Some women from the brothel were on their way back from El-Hamel. Painted and bedecked, they were rather pretty, and came to have a cigarette with us. Did fantasias in their honour all along the way. Laughed a lot ...

The legend of El-Hamel's pilgrims appeals to my imagination. It must be one of Algeria's most biblical stories ...

I began this diary over in that hated land of exile, during one of the blackest and most painfully uncertain periods in my life, a time fraught with suffering of every sort. Today it is coming to an end.

Everything is radically different now, myself included.

I have now been back in blessed Africa for a whole year, and hope to never leave it again. However poor, I have been able to travel and explore uncharted places in my adopted land ... My Ouïha is alive, and materially speaking, we are relatively well off ...

This diary, begun a year and a half ago in horrible Marseilles, comes to an end today, while the weather is grey and transparent, soft and almost dreamy here in Bou-Saada, another Southern spot I used to yearn for over there!

I am getting used to this tiny room of mine at the Moorish bath; it is so much like me and the way I live. I will be living in it for a few more days before setting off on my journey to Boghar, through areas I have never seen: a poorly whitewashed rectangle, a tiny window giving out on the mountains and the street, two mats on the floor, a line on which to hang my laundry, and the small torn mattress I am sitting on as I write. In one corner lie straw baskets; in the opposite one is the fireplace; my papers lie scattered about ... And that is all. For me, that will do.

There is no more than a vague echo in these pages of all that has happened these last eighteen months; I have filled them at random, whenever I have felt the need to *articulate* ... For the uninitiated reader, these pages would hardly make much sense. For myself they are a vestige of my earlier cult of the past. The day may come perhaps when I will no longer record the odd thought and impression in order to make them last a while. For the moment, I sometimes find great solace in re-reading these words about days gone by.

I shall start another diary. What shall I record there, and where shall I be, the day in the distant future when I shall be closing it, the way I am closing this one today?
'Allah knows what is hidden and the measure of people's sincerity!'

Isabelle Eberhardt was killed in a flood at Aïn-Sefra on 21 October 1904, nine months after this last entry in her journal.

NOTES

1 Isabelle's mother, born Nathalie Eberhardt, illegitimate daughter of Nicolas Korff and Fraulein Eberhardt, whose name she was given. She married General Paul de Moerder, a Russian nobleman and officer in Tsar Alexander's Imperial Army, by whom she had two sons and a daughter – Nicolas, Nathalie and Vladimir – before running off with her children's tutor, Alexander Trophimovsky, with whom she settled in Geneva, and by whom she had a son and a daughter – Augustin and Isabelle (who was registered in her maiden name). Madame de Moerder inherited the General's wealth, with which she subsidised her Geneva household. She became a convert to Islam, and died in Bône in Algeria, where she had gone to live with Isabelle.

2 Isabelle's brother Augustin, with whom she was thought to have been in love. It is not altogether clear whether Augustin was the son of General de Moerder (who recognised him, giving him his name) or of Trophimovsky. In any event, both he and Isabelle grew up believing that they were the children of a deceased Russian nobleman, and were never informed that Trophimovsky was their actual father.

3 Eugène Letord, a French Lieutenant attached to the Arab Bureau in South Constantine, with whom Isabelle corresponded in response to a request advertised in a newspaper. He was the first to suggest to her that she might establish herself in North Africa. He remained a good friend to her throughout her life, and may have been, for a brief period at least, her lover as well.

4 The name of the house in Geneva where Isabelle was born, bought with Madame de Moerder's money which had been left her by the General.

5 Alexander Trophimovsky, Isabelle's father (although unknown to her as such; she and Augustin referred to him as 'Vava', or 'Great-Uncle'). He was of Armenian origin, an ex-pope of the Russian Orthodox Church, an anarchist, a gifted scholar and a linguist. Engaged by the General as a tutor

to his sons, Trophimovsky instead became a lover to his wife.

6 Rehid Bey, a young diplomat of Armenian origin, who was attached to the Turkish Consulate in Geneva when Isabelle was in her late teens. He was a cultured man and an enlightened Muslim, who instructed his willing pupil in religious matters, and made passionate love to her. She called him 'Archivir', and he was to figure in her emotional life for several years to come.

7 The graves of her father, Alexander Trophimovsky, and of her half-brother, Vladimir de Moerder, at Vernier in Switzerland.

8 The Muslim cemetery in Bône where Madame de Moerder was buried.

9 Quoted from Pierre Loti's, *Le Mariage de Loti*

10 Isabelle's mother.

11 Archivir had by now been transferred to a posting in Paris.

12 Isabelle later wrote in the margin: 'In memory of that fateful date, 16 June 1900. That is how my fate was sealed, either by some unconscious mechanism or by pure inspiration. From the recesses of my soul came all of a sudden a picture of the road to be followed, the very road that was to lead me to the Bir Arbi garden and to Slimène, to the khouans, Behima, and salvation.' Marseilles, 23 July 1901.

13 Quoted from the *Journal des Goncourts*, Vol II.

14 An unfinished novel which Isabelle wrote, found among her papers at the time of her death, but rendered almost illegible from the effects of the flood which took her life.

15 All that we have of this is a fragment.

16 Quoted from the *Journal des Goncourts*, Vol III.

17 Isabelle later wrote in the margin: 'A few days later, the Mektoub saw to it that my lot was tied to Slimène's for ever.'

18 Written in the margin in 1901: 'My faith comes first, my Art comes next, and that will do, for those are the productive forces that embrace all of the universe.'

19 In the margin: 'The only thing that makes sense is the written word.'

20 Eugène Letord.

21 Isabelle left Marseilles on 21 July 1900, on board the SS *Eugène Pereire*. She arrived in Algiers at 3 p.m. the next day.

22 Isabelle noted in the margin: 'There was a French soldier there who had turned up from nowhere.'

23 This is Isabelle's first mention of Slimène Ehnni, a quartermaster of the Spahis, whose acquaintance she made one evening in the cool garden at Bir Arbi, and who was to become

her husband. She refers to him as 'Rouh', 'Zouizou', and 'Ouïha Kahla'.

24 Isabelle noted in the margin: 'A year's span! A year has gone by, and my life is linked to his for ever!'

25 Sidi Hussein ben Brahim, mokkadem of the zawyia of Guemar, and one of the sons of the venerated marabout and grand sheikh of the Kadrya confraternity, the late Sidi Brahim. Isabelle received her initiation into the sect through Sidi Hussein, who was impressed with her devotion, but who also thought that she might prove useful to him with the French authorities, with whom he believed she was affiliated.

26 Isabelle noted in the margin on 22 December 1900: 'A few days later, the house where we had that siesta was ravaged by typhus, which killed five people.'

27 Sidi Mahmoud Lachmi, brother of Sidi Hussein, son of Sidi Brahim, sheikh of the Kadryas. Si Lachmi had managed to impose himself as Grand Master of the Order, despite the fact that many refused to consider him as a marabout since his reputation for double-dealing and for scandal detracted from his powers of spiritual leadership. Isabelle fell under his powerful spell, becoming his sometime mistress and secretary.

28 The man who tried to kill Isabelle at Behima.

29 The day that Slimène was to be discharged.

30 Augustin wrote to Isabelle, thus making a gesture of accepting her union with Slimène, of which he had disapproved initially.

31 A French police officer.

32 The Tidjanya was an Algerian confraternity thought to be an ally of the French; it was hostile to the Kadrya confraternity to which Isabelle belonged.

33 Women were not allowed into the promiscuity of the fourth-class compartment, and Isabelle, who could not afford to travel in better style, was forced to disguise herself as a deck-hand.

34 Perhaps Isabelle had a premonition of her future death by drowning.

35 Dr Grenier was a former member of the French Parliament for the Doubs province, who paraded in native dress, claiming to be a Muslim for political reasons.

36 There is strong disagreement on this point. Some observers believed that the assassin actually belonged to the Kadrya confraternity, and had been ordered by Si Lachmi himself to do away with Isabelle, since the latter had tired of the mistress who had proved an embarrassment to him, especially as she wielded no power whatsoever with the French, contrary to what he had been led to suppose. But the case remains

mysterious, especially as accounts of it were suppressed at the time in the French North African press.

37 A descendant of the Prophet Muhammad, and thus a highly regarded notable.

38 Isabelle did in fact recover full use of her arm.

39 This was one of the explanations offered then. The Tidjanyas were thought to be in the pocket of the French, who did not much care for Isabelle during this period (although they were to find her quite useful at a later stage).

40 Some of Isabelle's more patronising sentiments. She was a colonial at heart, and something of an apologist for French rule in North Africa, which she believed to be both beneficial and benign.

41 During Isabelle's first journey to North Africa, she made a number of excursions on horseback into the Tunisian Sahel.

42 No sooner had the verdict been announced [twenty years of hard labour for Isabelle's assailant] than she was expelled from the country.

43 Sidi Lachmi.

44 A female marabout, a holy woman. In this fantasy, Isabelle was presuming a great deal about her status in North Africa. It is very difficult to believe that her aspiration to become a spiritual leader – the aspiration of a promiscuous foreign woman masquerading as a boy, and a penniless and power-less one at that – could have ever been taken seriously by a hierarchical religious society such as that of the confra-ternities, where maraboutism was on the whole an inherited spiritual and political eminence.

45 Madam de Moerder's money in Russia, left to her by the General on condition it be applied for in person at regular in-tervals. The question of this inheritance was appallingly mis-handled, so that Isabelle never managed to benefit from it at all.

46 In her brother Augustin's impoverished household in Marseilles.

47 Her half-brother Vladimir, who committed suicide in the Villa Neuve in Geneva.

48 Augustin's little daughter, Hélène.

49 Two pieces that Isabelle wrote in the hopes of finding a publisher.

50 After her expulsion from Algeria, Slimène went back to his barracks where he fell seriously ill. The letters he wrote to Isabelle at that time were those of a desperate man.

51 Slimène.

52 In fact, Slimène managed to recover from this bout of tuberculosis.

53 Editors who found Isabelle some work in journalism.
54 French doctor who cared for Isabelle after she was wounded at Behima. He was something of an anarchist himself, and a sensualist, and at some point in their acquaintance he and Isabelle had an affair.
55 Another of Isabelle's lovers.
56 A French officer who became Isabelle's lover.
57 Isabelle travelled to Geneva for ten days on 21 December.
58 The first time she actually meets Victor Barrucand, who was to be a help to her for the remainder of her life, finding her work and defending her interests, as well as those of Slimène. He would also edit her work for publication after her death.
59 Reflective of Isabelle's rather contradictory reaction to place.
60 An influential holy woman, a maraboute.
61 Sidi Embarek, another of the influential figures of the Kadrya.
62 A comment reflective of Isabelle's dislike of women.
63 The French Orientalist and writer, better known by his pen-name of Robert Randau, who had taken up an official post in the French colonial administration. He and Isabelle became firm friends, and he later wrote his recollections of her.
64 A nationalist revolt against the French in which a group of North Africans attempted to destabilise colonial rule by attacking a French garrison.
65 Although Brieux encouraged Isabelle to write about this subject, she never did, perhaps not wishing to offend the French colonial authorities.
66 L'Oeil du monde, one of the most spectacular peaks in the Algerian Atlas Mountains.
67 The Muslim month of fasting.

GLOSSARY

asr	afternoon, and afternoon prayer
bach-adel	notary
bach-hamar	head of donkey- or camel-drivers
benadir	chants
bendar	drum
borj	outpost building
burnous	traditional North African cape with hood, worn by men
caïd	notable, leader
chaouch	policeman
chechiya	headdress
chih	fragrant plant
ch'ile	torch
chira	variety of marijuana
deïra	head of locality
dikr	short prayer
diss	herb
djérid	palm leaves
dolce far niente	sweet do-nothingness
doum	herb
drinn	shrub
fajr	dawn, also morning prayer
fatiha	opening verse of the Quran
fellah	peasant
gasba	flute
gourbi	shanty town
guerbas	waterskins
habous	concierge
hakkam	ruler (referring to the French *colon*)
hamel	porter
hendie	cactus
icha	evening, the evening prayer
jujube	shrub
kabal	tribe
kachébia	Arab cloak

kenoun	coal brazier
kepi	cap
keram	fig tree
khammesat	agricultural system, whereby the peasant receives only one-fifth of the produce of the land he has worked
khouans	initiates in a confraternity
kif	literally meaning 'high', in this case referring to whatever induces the state: marijuana or tobacco
koubba	dome
ksar	county
ksour	counties
maghreb	literally, 'where the sun sets', but also meaning the time of day it sets, twilight, and the maghreb prayer
maghreb eddan	twilight call to prayer
maquis	bush, scrub (but also the anti-French Resistance Movement)
marabout	holy man
mechta	area surrounding the gourbi shanty
medha	religious ceremony of praise
mektoub	literally, 'that which is written', i.e. fate or destiny
mihrab	altar
misbahs	lamps
mokkadem	local sheikh
moucharabieh	carved wooden shutters
naib	delegate of a sheikh in a confraternity
nefsaoua des bendar	dervishes with drums
oued	valley, stream, ravine or river bed
oumara	vessel
roumi	literally 'Roman', but also Christian, western, etc.
sehkha	salt lake
segniyas	place where arms are kept
seguia	drinking bottle or pitcher
sekakri	seller of sweetmeats
sherif	descendant of the Prophet, a notable

115

shott	salt lake
shurafa	plural of sherif; notables
sobh	morning
souafa	connected to holy or burial ground
taam	feast
talba	student, initiate
tarika	holy sect
thujas	fragrant flowering plant
tolbas	students or seekers
toub	mud
wakil	keeper of the mosque
zawyia	home of marabouts, also serving as a school of theology and law, as a haven where students rest and persecuted men find sanctuary
zeriba	a sty or stable where livestock is kept
ziara	pilgrimage
zorna	flutes